Portrait of Francisco Vásquez de Coronado, by Bill Ahrendt

THE WORLD'S GREAT EXPLORERS

Francisco de Coronado

By R. Conrad Stein

CHILDRENS PRESS ®

CHICAGO

The Petrified Forest of northeast-
ern Arizona, part of the Painted
Desert through which Coronado's
men marched

Project Editor: Ann Heinrichs
Designer: Lindaanne Donohoe
Cover Art: Steven Gaston Dobson
Engraver: Liberty Photoengraving

Library of Congress
Cataloging-in-Publication Data

Stein, R. Conrad.
   Francisco de Coronado / by R. Conrad Stein.
      p.   cm. — (The World's great explorers)
   Includes bibliographical references and index.
   Summary: Describes Coronado's explorations in the
southwestern United States in the 1540s, an expedition which revealed for the first time to Europeans the
Grand Canyon, the Painted Desert, the Great Plains,
herds of buffalo, stark deserts, snow-capped mountain
peaks—yet never the gold the Spaniards so avidly
desired.
   ISBN 0-516-03068-X
   1. Coronado, Francisco Vásquez de, 1510-1554—
Juvenile literature. 2. Southwest, New—Discovery
and exploration—Spanish—Juvenile literature 3.
Explorers—America—Biography—Juvenile literature.
4. Explorers—Spain—Biography—Juvenile literature.
[1. Coronado, Francisco Vásquez de, 1510-1554. 2.
Explorers. 3. Southwest, New—Discovery and
exploration. 4. America—Discovery and exploration.]
I. Title. II. Series.
E125.V3S74 1992
917.604 '1' 092—dc20
[B]

91-32207
CIP
AC

Coronado erecting a cross at the Arkansas River

Table of Contents

Chapter 1
An Expedition Begins

The village of Compostela in western Mexico was a collection of twenty adobe houses lining a dusty, wind-blown street. It was a humble place for launching a history-making expedition. Yet, in February 1540, the villagers watched some three hundred Spanish soldiers assume a parade formation. All night the troops had polished their weapons to look smart for the event. One foot soldier, Pedro de Castañeda, later wrote that the men formed "the most brilliant company ever assembled to go in search of new lands."

Antonio de Mendoza

Bidding the army farewell was Antonio de Mendoza, the viceroy of New Spain (present-day Mexico). He had traveled 500 miles (805 kilometers) from New Spain's capital, Mexico City, to wish the Spaniards good fortune on their exploration mission. Before the march began, the viceroy presided over a swearing-in ceremony. Each Spaniard placed his hand on a cross and took a solemn oath "to uphold the service of God and his Majesty and to be obedient to [the commander] Francisco Vásquez de Coronado." Then the soldiers faced north. Amid the blasts of bugles and the rolling beats of drums, they began their march into the unknown.

Spanish soldiers led the procession. Behind them paraded an army of eight hundred Indian allies and a small contingent of black slaves. Some of the men

Coronado mural by Gerald Cassidy in the Museum of New Mexico

tended to the thousand or more horses and mules that served as pack animals. Still others herded flocks of sheep, goats, and pigs that were expected to provide meat for the expedition members.

Riding at the head of the long column was Coronado, a twenty-nine-year-old Spanish nobleman. His orders were to trek into the wilderness to the north of New Spain's frontier. No large group of Spaniards had ventured into this land before. It was believed that the north was resplendent with wondrous cities rich in gold.

Coronado rode his horse ramrod straight, the perfect picture of a Spanish commander. If he felt a twinge of fear at challenging the unexplored land ahead, he buried the emotion. He was one of the Spanish *conquistadores* (conquerors), the bravest men of a brave nation.

Chapter 2
God, Gold, and Glory

"We Spaniards suffer from a disease of the heart which can only be cured by gold."

—*Hernando Cortés, the conqueror of Mexico*

Spain was a breeding ground for warriors. For seven hundred years, the men of Spain fought the Moors who had marched up from North Africa and occupied their land. Then, in 1492, two events brought peace to an embattled Spain and raised the nation to the ranks of a world power. First, Spanish forces captured the city of Granada, the last bastion of the Moors in Spain. Second, the Spanish monarchs King Ferdinand and Queen Isabella sent the Italian captain, Christopher Columbus, on a voyage to find a new sea route to spice-rich Asian lands. Columbus failed to reach Asia, but he planted the Spanish flag in a new land on the Caribbean Sea that was previously unknown to Europeans.

Spanish adventurers flocked to the Caribbean islands Columbus had discovered. They occupied the island of Hispaniola (present-day Haiti and the Dominican Republic), and soon afterward explored and conquered the neighboring island of Cuba. The Spaniards were ruthless in their treatment of the native Caribbean people. Spain at that time was a cruel society where men and women were subjected to terrible tortures and were commonly put to death by being burned at the stake. The Spanish conquistadores brought these Old World horrors to the New World.

In 1519, the Spaniard Hernando Cortés took an army of five hundred soldiers to the shores of Mexico. Cortés, the greatest conquistador of them all, defeated the mighty Aztec empire and claimed Mexico for the Spanish king. Victory followed victory for the conquistadores. By 1540—less than five decades after

Hernando Cortés battling Mexico's Aztec Indians

Columbus's first voyage—the Spanish flag flew from outposts ranging from Hispaniola west to Mexico and south to Peru. Millions of Indian people had fallen under Spanish rule.

Also in the early 1500s, the Portuguese explored and placed colonies in what is now Brazil. Far to the north, the French sailed into the St. Lawrence River, which today flows between eastern Canada and the United States, and laid claim to that region. The English and the Dutch came later to carve out their portions of the American continent. But no European power claimed more of the New World than did Spain.

During the course of their expansion, the Spaniards undertook heroic exploration missions. Neither thick jungles nor towering mountains nor hostile natives deterred them from their goal. But their expeditions sought more than the discovery of new lands.

Historians have summed up Spanish presence in the Americas in three words: God, gold, and glory. The warriors sought glory on the battlefield. Nurtured by seven centuries of almost constant warfare, the Spanish soldier looked upon the battlefield as a glorious proving ground where boys became men and the boldest of fighters became heroes. In addition to their zest for war, the Spaniards believed it was their holy duty to carry the word of Christ to the people of the Americas. So zealous were the conquistadores about saving Indian souls that they were willing to torture and murder those who resisted converting to Christianity. Finally, the Spaniards, like most Europeans of the era, possessed a burning hunger for gold. Not only did gold bring comfort in this world, but it was also believed that enough coins donated to the church would assure a man a lofty place in heaven.

Gold ornament of the Mixtec Indians, found in the Monte Alban site in Oaxaca, Mexico

Early in the age of exploration, which began after Columbus's discoveries, Spain was haunted by legends of vast riches to be found in the Americas. It was said that cities existed in the New World where even the poorest people ate from solid gold plates. Children in those cities used huge gold objects as toys. In two instances, the tales of New World wealth proved true. Hernando Cortés sacked the Aztec treasury and seized gold, silver, and rare gems worth a fortune. An even bigger haul was gained by the conquistador Francisco Pizarro, who crushed the Incas in Peru and discovered their mountain castles contained large rooms piled to the ceiling with gold and silver.

The Aztec capital city of Tenochtitlán, where Mexico City stands today, as painted by Mexican artist Diego Rivera

The most persistent Spanish story of New World riches involved seven mysterious bishops. The story told of a time four hundred years before Columbus, when the Moors still occupied Spain. According to the legend, seven Spanish bishops escaped Moorish rule by building boats and crossing the Sea of Darkness (the Atlantic Ocean). After braving the ocean, they encountered a fruitful land they called Antilia. In the new land they found rivers of golden sand. They built seven cities, one for each bishop. Houses in the cities were made from pure gold, the most common material Antilia had to offer. The Spaniards believed the bishops' seven cities lay somewhere beyond the northern frontiers of New Spain.

Only a bold explorer could search the unknown land and discover the fabled cities. Finding the seven cities of treasure was the task of General Francisco Vásquez de Coronado. He seemed to be the perfect man for the job.

Coronado was born in 1510 in Salamanca, a university town in the Spanish province of Leon. He came from a family of noblemen who were friends of the Spanish monarchs. No portrait of Coronado was made in his lifetime, but he was said to have been a handsome youth. Though he was raised in a huge house and was attended by servants, Coronado still suffered from an accident of birth: He was one of the younger sons in his family. Spanish law decreed that a father's estate go entirely to the oldest son. When the father died, Coronado would be left with a pitifully small portion of the family's holdings.

Young Coronado decided to seek his fortune in the New World. Hundreds of other young Spanish noblemen had come to the same decision. The Caribbean islands and New Spain were overrun with men of high birth who had little money but were too proud to work. A Spanish priest wrote bitterly about this idle class: "They do nothing but command. . . . They come out very poor from Spain, carrying only their sword. But in a year they have gotten together more goods than a drove of animals can carry, and they insist on having the houses of gentlemen."

Before leaving home, Coronado made an important friend in Antonio de Mendoza, who was also from Salamanca. A member of one of Spain's highest-ranking families, Mendoza had recently been appointed viceroy of New Spain. A viceroy had authority second only to that of the king, Charles I of Spain. By declaring Mendoza viceroy, the Spanish monarch sent a message that the freebooting conquistador era was at an end. King Charles I feared that the early conquistadores, such as Cortés, desired to carve out empires for themselves instead of claiming land for the Spanish government. Mendoza was of a new breed of official, obedient and fiercely loyal to the king.

Mendoza and Coronado arrived together in New Spain in 1535. They established homes in Mexico City. Just fifteen years earlier, Mexico City was the site of the glorious Aztec capital called Tenochtitlan. A titanic battle was fought there between the Aztecs and the conquistadores led by Cortés. Now a new Spanish city rose over the ruins of the old Aztec capital.

In Mexico City, Coronado quickly climbed the political and social ladder. Mendoza gave him a seat on the Mexico City Municipal Council. Two years after he arrived, Coronado married Beatríz de Estrada, who was perhaps the wealthiest woman in New Spain. Next, Mendoza ordered Coronado to put down a rebel-

Detail of a Mexican painting showing early contact between the Spaniards and the Indians

One of the mines that Spaniards operated in Mexico, using native people as slaves

lion among Indians and black slaves who had taken over a silver mine. Coronado handled the assignment admirably. Mendoza then named Coronado the governor of New Galicia province, which was north and west of Mexico City. The tiny village of Compostela, from which Coronado's history-making mission was launched, served as New Galicia's capital.

As governor of New Galicia, Coronado remained Viceroy Mendoza's right-hand man. He enjoyed the wealth he gained through his marriage to Beatríz de Estrada. The stage was set for the most impressive act of Coronado's career. Mendoza believed that no one was more qualified to lead an army of men on an exploration mission to the north. That land, though shrouded with mystery, had been seen by a handful of Spaniards.

Chapter 3
Before Coronado

"The story of Cabeza de Vaca is incredible, and would have to be considered myth except that it is true."

—Bernard de Voto, from his book The Course of Empire

Alvar Núñez Cabeza de Vaca was a Spanish nobleman who journeyed to Cuba early in the age of exploration. In 1528 he set out, with three hundred Spaniards, on an ill-fated exploration mission to Florida. Their ship was washed ashore by storms, and many of the men were killed by hostile natives. The survivors built horse-hide rafts and tried to float back to Cuba. Most of the Spaniards drowned. Cabeza de Vaca drifted to a sandy island that most historians believe to be Galveston Island off the coast of Texas. He was promptly captured by Indians and made a slave.

Eventually Cabeza de Vaca escaped from his slave masters and hiked inland. He learned Indian ways and became a trader. As he relentlessly walked through the wilderness, he exchanged colorful seashells he had found on the coast for food with tribes that lived many miles from the sea. During his trading adventures he met three other surviving members of his shipwrecked crew. One of the survivors was Estéban, a black slave from North Africa. Estéban would later play a key role in the Spanish exploration of the land north of New Spain.

Cabeza de Vaca and his companions living among the Indians

The four men decided to march west, toward the setting sun. They hoped to run into the Pacific shore and then turn south to link up with an outpost in New Spain. Their journey was incredible, carrying them through the untamed regions of what is now Texas, New Mexico, and Arizona. Nomadic Indians served as their guides. In the vast deserts, the four learned how to survive on the fruits of the prickly-pear cactus. An occasional deer, felled by Indian bowmen, provided a feast.

As they traveled from one tribal territory to another, they earned reputations as powerful medicine men. No one knows how or why the local people came to believe the strangers possessed extraordinary healing powers. The four outsiders examined sick people and mimicked tribal medicine men by chanting and

Cabeza de Vaca and his men treating the Indians' illnesses

by blowing on the afflicted areas of people's bodies. The native Americans had no idea the four were simply chanting the Catholic prayers they had learned as boys. Their special magic must have worked, because appreciative Indians heaped gifts upon the foreigners. The Pima people of what is now southern Arizona gave Cabeza de Vaca five highly valued ceremonial arrowheads made of a sparkling green stone.

The dark-skinned Estéban was especially revered as a healer. One tribe presented Estéban with a rattle made of a gourd. Distant tribes swooned in awe when Estéban rattled the gourd over men and women to chase the sicknesses out of them. Estéban also enjoyed the gift of languages. As the four men wandered, he quickly learned complex tribal dialects and served as the group's interpreter.

Cabeza de Vaca crossing North America's deserts and plains

Word of the marvelous powers possessed by Cabeza de Vaca and his band of healers raced ahead of their path. Tribes welcomed the medicine men, giving them beans, pumpkins, and blankets made from deer hide. Cabeza de Vaca wrote that one family "offered us all they had as well as their house." But the foreigners had become discouraged. They had roamed the country ceaselessly and seemed nowhere near their goal.

After many weary months, Cabeza de Vaca and his party crossed the Rio Grande somewhere near present-day El Paso, Texas. At the Yaqui River in what is now northern Mexico, they spotted an Indian wearing a curious object on his belt. Upon closer examination, they discovered the object was a Spanish-made horseshoe nail. Finally the men knew they were near Spanish civilization.

The odyssey of Cabeza de Vaca ended in 1536, when he and a group of Indian guides met a Spaniard in northwestern Mexico. The amazing journey had lasted eight years and covered some 6,000 miles (9,656 kilometers). Yet Cabeza de Vaca's encounter with his first representative of New Spain was filled with irony. The Spaniard he met was a lieutenant of a brutal conquistador named Nuño de Guzmán, who earned a fortune enslaving Indians. The lieutenant was on a slave-gathering mission when he chanced into the wandering party. During his long journey, Cabeza de Vaca had learned to respect and even to love the Indian people. When the lieutenant attempted to capture his guides, the exhausted Spanish officer forbade him even to touch the men.

The Rio Grande

Mexico City around the year 1673

In Mexico City, Cabeza de Vaca and his fellow travelers were greeted as heroes. Viceroy Mendoza questioned the men carefully. Was there any evidence of gold in the north? Had they seen or heard of the fabulously wealthy cities that legends claimed were founded by the seven bishops centuries earlier?

Cabeza de Vaca told the viceroy he had seen no large cities. But he did offer rumors he had heard while living among the Indian people. Various tribal leaders had told him that far to the north, beyond the mountains and deserts, were wealthy nations whose citizens lived in huge houses and where emeralds, turquoises, and other rare gems lay about the ground, common as stones. In a written account, Cabeza de Vaca told of the gifts presented to him by the Pima people who lived in present-day Arizona: "To me they gave five emeralds made into arrowheads, which they used at singing and dancing. . . . I asked them where they got these; and they said the stones were brought from some lofty mountains that stand toward the north, where there were populous towns and large houses."

Cabeza de Vaca's report electrified Mexico City. True, he had personally seen no evidence of great wealth in the north. The stories he told were based on secondhand information he had heard from tribal leaders. Also, it was never established that the green arrowheads given him by the Pima people were genuine emeralds; they could have been any variety of lesser stone. Nevertheless, Cabeza de Vaca's probe into the northland set the Spaniards dreaming of treasure troves to rival those found by Cortés and Pizarro.

Viceroy Mendoza was a cautious man. Like most Spaniards, he believed in the existence of seven great cities founded by the Christian bishops. North of the New Spain frontier was a logical place for the cities to stand, since that was the least explored region in the Americas. Still, he wanted to be sure of the cities' location before sending out a major expedition. The viceroy summoned a Franciscan priest named Marcos de Niza, known as Fray Marcos. The priest had traveled with the conquistadores in Peru and was known to be a fearless explorer. Fray Marcos was ordered to take a small party to the northland and make contact with the residents of the great cities. Mendoza appointed the slave Estéban to act as his guide.

Foremost on the viceroy's mind was finding the seven cities. But Mendoza also had an intellectual curiosity about new lands. He told Fray Marcos to study "the people who are there, if they be many or few . . . the quality and fertility of the soil, the temperature of the country, the trees and plants and domestic and feral animals which may be there; the rivers, if they are large or small, and the minerals or metals which are there." The belief that somewhere a sea route ran through the North American continent was still strong among Europeans. The viceroy ordered Niza to study all prominent rivers, "because some arm of the sea may enter the land beyond."

Marcos de Niza, Estéban, and a troop of Indians began their expedition in the spring of 1539. Key to the mission's success was Estéban. Though he was technically still a slave, he had a firsthand knowledge of the land and a unique ability to master native languages. Estéban relished his role as a leader. He wore a bright-colored robe and a hat adorned with rare feathers. Always at his side was the rattle that had so bedazzled villagers during his previous wanderings in the north.

Estéban served as point man, leading a troop of Indians that hiked many miles ahead of Niza and the main party. In order that Estéban could report what he saw, he and the priest worked out a simple code. When Estéban spotted an Indian community, he was to send back a runner bearing a cross. The larger the cross, the larger the settlement.

As the main body marched north and approached what is now the state line of New Mexico, Fray Marcos was shocked to see a messenger approaching him staggering under the weight of a huge cross. The runner

Estéban on the Marcos de Niza expedition, as shown in a watercolor by Michael Waters

told the priest that Estéban had learned of a marvelous country that held many large and splendid cities. The slave had not seen the land, but Indians they had met swore it was just up ahead. The natives said the rich country was called Cíbola. Fray Marcos repeated the name, "Cíbola." The word would soon work magic with the adventurers of New Spain.

Marcos de Niza quickened his pace, eager to see this magnificent land. Other messengers reported in, carrying even more encouraging news. They claimed that Cíbola had seven major cities, just as the legends said. Then, in late May 1539, the priest received tragic tidings. Two messengers arrived covered with wounds. They said that when Estéban and his Indian troop approached the first city of Cíbola, they were attacked and the slave was killed. Estéban's gourd held no power over these people.

Scene in New Mexico of the Rio Grande with the Sandia Mountains in the background

The priest grimly pushed on, hoping at least to catch sight of this great city. Considering Estéban's fate, Fray Marcos had no desire to get too close. From a hill rising in present-day New Mexico, he looked down and beheld what he believed to be a vast city. Surely this metropolis was the fulfillment of a legend. Niza turned and hurried back to Mexico City.

At the headquarters of Viceroy Mendoza, the priest presented a written statement: "The settlement [I saw] is larger than the city of Mexico. At times I was tempted to go to it, because I knew that I risked only my life, and this I had offered to God the day I began the expedition. But the fact is that I was afraid . . . that if I should die it would not be possible to have an account of this land, which, in my opinion, is the largest and best of all those yet discovered."

The words "larger than the city of Mexico" astounded Mendoza. Mexico City of old—before Cortés defeated the Aztecs—was a vast metropolis, resplendent with pyramids and elegant homes. It held a quarter of a million people, making it perhaps the biggest city in the world. And Marcos de Niza's report was even more enticing when he referred to another country, called Abra, which he had heard about during his travels: "I heard that there is much gold, and the natives of Abra make it into vessels, and ornaments for the ears, and utensils with which they scrape themselves to remove the sweat."

Marcos de Niza's account of his journey to the north added fuel to the excitement already raging in Mexico City. A Spaniard had found the seven cities! The seven cities had a name: Cíbola, Cíbola, Cíbola! The single word was on the lips of every Spaniard.

Drawing of Marcos de Niza

Chapter 4
The Trek North

From every corner of Mexico, Spaniards scrambled to join the search for the seven magnificent cities. Some of the eager recruits had to be turned away. Finally a company made up of three hundred of the finest men was chosen.

There was never any doubt that Coronado was to command the mission. He was the personal choice of Viceroy Mendoza. Also, the two men shared in the cost of equipping the venture. Mendoza spent 60,000 Spanish ducats and Coronado put up 50,000 ducats. In today's money, that sum would total more than two million dollars. Coronado's share came from the sizable fortune he had gained by marrying Doña Beatríz de Estrada.

*Drawing of a Spanish conquistador
in full military gear*

Both Mendoza and Coronado believed the treasure to be found by the expedition would more than return their investments. Under Spanish law, one-fifth of all the gold and silver taken on the venture had to go to the king. That amount was called the "king's fifth." The remainder of the treasure was to be divided among the officers, the men, and the financial backers.

Coronado recruited his soldiers in Mexico City and various other parts of New Spain. The men were young, many still in their teens. Most were of noble birth but lacked money of their own. New Spain had hundreds of these young blades, and all hoped to reap rewards like those the earlier conquistadores had won. Often these youthful aristocrats—who refused to do any form of manual labor—spent their time in Mexico City

Coronado's march

drinking, gambling, and fighting duels over the few
Spanish women who were available. Once his army
was assembled, Coronado led the men on a long hike
to the frontiers of New Galicia and into the village of
Compostela. One Mexico City resident was glad to see
this band of fortune hunters march off, claiming they
were "vicious young men with nothing to do."

Accompanying the Coronado party were five
Franciscan priests. It was hoped that their presence
would protect the Indians of the north from brutality
at the hands of the soldiers. Earlier contacts between
the Spanish army and New World civilizations re-
sulted in terrible destruction. The bishop of Mexico
City had urged the priests to make sure the conquest
of the northern lands be "Christian and not a butchery."

Prominent among the priests was Marcos de Niza, who served as a guide as well as a spiritual counselor. In private conversations, Niza had told incredible stories about the riches to be found in the north. His barber claimed the priest said, "[In Cíbola] the cities were surrounded by walls, with their gates guarded, and were very wealthy, having silversmiths; and that the women wore strings of gold beads and the men girdles of gold." A fellow priest wrote, "The friar told me this, that he saw a temple of their idols, the walls of which, inside and outside, were covered with precious stones; I think he said they were emeralds."

Niza's stories fired the dreams of the young Spaniards who now marched with Coronado. They looked upon the north and Cíbola as another land similar to Mexico, which twenty years earlier overflowed with treasure. In their chattering, the soldiers called the north "un nuevo Mexico"—a new Mexico. Hence the region, and later an American state, acquired its name.

✳ ✳ ✳ ✳ ✳

Upon leaving Compostela, Coronado's army trudged north to Culiacán, the last outpost in the northern New Spain frontier. Before arriving at the village, the men received disheartening news. Months earlier, Viceroy Mendoza had sent Melchor Díaz, an experienced scout, to the north to find out what lay ahead for Coronado. Díaz entered the Spanish camp and told the commander that much of the land to the north was not green and fruitful, as Fray Marcos had reported. Many miles ahead lay a sprawling *despoblado*—an uninhabited wilderness—where food was nonexistent. Also, Díaz had spoken to many Indians who said they knew of no gold in the north. Coronado ordered Melchor Díaz to keep his news a secret from

Desert scenery near Hermosillo in Sonora state, northern Mexico

the men. But Díaz's silence only aroused the soldiers' suspicions.

The huge column of Spaniards and Indian allies inched its way north. Herding the sheep and other animals the army brought for food was a painfully slow process. When the men encountered deep rivers, the sheep had to be carried across by hand. At the outpost of Culiacán, Coronado decided the expedition was moving too slowly. The commander announced he would lead a party of eighty Spanish horsemen, twenty-five Spanish foot soldiers, and a contingent of Indian allies on a fast march to Cíbola. The main body of soldiers would begin to build base camps in what is now northern Mexico.

After several weeks of travel, Coronado's party encountered more evidence of Marcos de Niza's lies. The army reached an Indian settlement called Chichilticalli, which, according to Niza's accounts, was a thriving town. Instead, the foot soldier Castañeda wrote, "The men were all disillusioned to see that the famous Chichilticalli turned out to be a roofless, ruined house." Earlier the soldiers had entered a valley that the priest had praised as the land of Abra, saying it contained gold and large cities. They found Abra to be an uninviting region that sustained only a few muddy villages.

In a letter to Viceroy Mendoza, a frustrated Coronado complained about the priest's fabrications.

Desert scene, with Arizona's Pinaleno Mountains in the background

"The whole company felt disturbed at this, that a thing so much praised, and about which the father had said so much, should be found so very different; and the men began to think that all the rest would be likewise."

In late May of 1540, the travelers entered what is now the state of Arizona. Historians conclude they crossed the border between Mexico and the United States at a point just south of present-day Bisbee, Arizona. Dry grasses and cactuses prevailed over this land, while the sun burned mercilessly above. Southern Arizona is one of the hottest regions in the United States. Temperatures there commonly reach 110 degrees Fahrenheit (43 degrees Celsius).

View looking south into Mexico from Arizona's Coronado Peak

But as the men traveled, the landscape shifted from desert to forest. Much of the American Southwest is a vertical rather than a horizontal country. Mountaintops in the region are forest-covered, while desert grasses prevail below. The transition is often sudden, and the abrupt change from grasslands to towering trees amazes a traveler.

Coronado's route took him into the Gila Mountains, whose peaks were blanketed with towering ponderosa pines. Today Arizona's Route 666—called the Coronado Trail—twists through the heart of this Gila Mountain pine country. It is a spectacular drive, but because of the rugged mountains the road is fraught with dangerous hairpin turns.

In the Gila Mountains, Indian guides showed the Spaniards how to prepare pine nuts to eat. The Indians ground up the nuts and added a few drops of water until they formed a paste. The nut mixture was then molded by hand into tiny cakes. To the famished Spaniards, the pine nut cakes tasted delicious.

Without the assistance of Indian guides, Coronado's men would have perished, or at the very least been forced to turn back. Most of the Indians Coronado chose as guides were traders who knew the country well. They were paid in precious white man's goods, such as iron knives or colorful beads. The Spanish journals record only a few of the guides' names, but their expert guidance was essential for the Europeans' survival.

Leaving the pine forest, the army confronted the vast *despoblado* (empty land) that the scout Melchor Díaz had warned them about. The *despoblado* spread over the Colorado Plateau, which follows the course of the Little Colorado River. Even today, this harsh,

The Gila Mountains between Fort Apache and Fort Thomas, Arizona

rainless landscape discourages settlement. In Coronado's time, it was completely devoid of people. "We found no grass during the first days," Coronado wrote about his trek over the *despoblado*, "and we encountered more dangerous passages than we had previously experienced. The horses were so exhausted they could not endure it. . . . The way is very bad . . . through impassable mountains."

While making their miserable way through this wasteland, many soldiers cast angry stares at Fray Marcos de Niza. He had described this land as a well-watered forest abundant with deer, rabbits, and other game animals.

Finally the *despoblado* faded as the men climbed the White Mountains in eastern Arizona. To their great relief, mountain trails led them through a dark, cool pine forest. On today's map, they had entered Arizona's Apache-Sitgreaves National Forest. Their course then shifted to the east, toward what is now the New Mexico border.

The forest was an ideal spot for the men to find food, and they did catch some fine fish, "like those in Spain." But they made no great effort to hunt and feed their grumbling bellies. Gold fever now ruled their emotions. Soon they would reach the cities where children used gold blocks as toys. Their excitement rose when they approached a stream they called the Red River because of its rust-colored waters. Marcos de Niza told the men this river flowed into Cíbola. This time the soldiers believed the priest.

Morning in the White Mountains of Arizona

This map, published in 1884, shows various Indian pueblos of the Southwest. The Zuñi pueblo, in the Cíbola region, was known as Háwikuh in Coronado's time.

However, a new danger now loomed. In the *despoblado* the Spaniards encountered no sign of native people. But along the Red River the men saw campfires flickering in the distant mountains at night. Cíbola, it was believed, was a large city. And the people there had already shown their hostility toward outsiders. The residents of Cíbola had killed the slave Estéban, seemingly for no reason.

Near the borderline between the present-day states of Arizona and New Mexico, a scouting party encountered four Indians. The four made gestures of peace. Using sign language, they indicated they were a welcoming committee sent out by the chiefs of Cíbola. They claimed the people of the city were generous and would gladly feed all the men of the army. The half-starved Spaniards almost wept with joy.

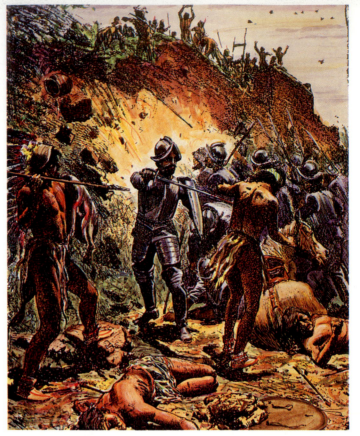

Spaniards fighting the Indians of New Mexico

Later that night, however, the hopes for a peaceful meeting between Spaniards and Cíbolans dissolved when a small force of Indians attacked a band of Coronado's men. The Indians were easily driven off, and they retreated, sounding a horn as they fled. The racket of the battle awoke the entire Spanish army. Around them the soldiers saw hills alive with camp-fires. Had they come this far, only to be killed in a nightmarish battle on the doorsteps of Cíbola?

The next morning Coronado ordered a quick march to Cíbola. He sensed his army faced combat. If Cíbola was indeed a city the size of old Mexico City, his men would be outnumbered by at least one hundred to one. Yet he hurried boldly forward. He had no other choice. As he later wrote, "We were in such great need of food that I thought we should all die of hunger if we

New Mexico's Zuñi Pueblo in the 1880s. Here once stood the village of Háwikuh, the first city of Cíbola that Coronado saw.

continued to be without provisions for another day. . . . So I was obliged to hasten forward without delay."

A path took the army onto a broad plain. Ahead the men caught their first glimpse of the silver city of Cíbola. As they marched closer, the soldiers were shocked. Where were the stately walls, studded with jewels? Where were the great pyramids that rose to the clouds? Instead of a magnificent metropolis, the Spaniards beheld a collection of stone houses ringed by a crude wall. It could hold eight hundred people at the most. Castañeda described it as "a small, rocky village, all crumped up." He added, "There are many farm settlements in New Spain that look far better."

Once more, all eyes turned to Marcos de Niza. "Such were the curses hurled at him," said Castañeda, "that I prayed God might protect him."

Chapter 5
In the Land of the Pueblos

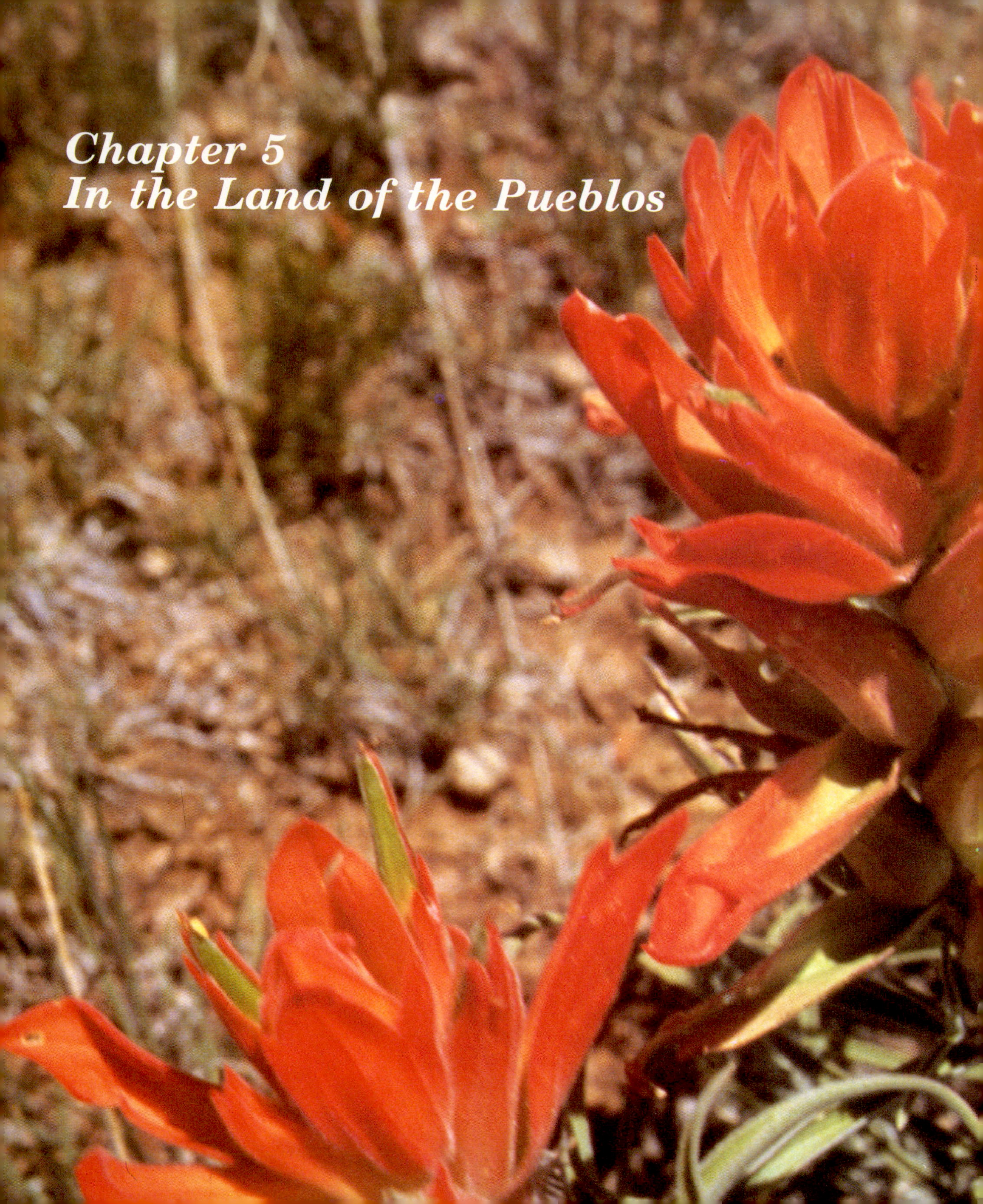

"They [the Pueblo people] do not have chiefs as in New Spain, but are ruled by a council of the oldest men. They have priests who preach to them. . . . They go up on the highest roof of the village and preach to the village from there, like public criers. In the morning while the sun is rising, the whole village is silent and sitting to listen."

Pedro de Castañeda, describing village routine in the land of the Pueblos

Coronado's army had reached the village of Háwikuh, part of the land area called Cíbola. The village was situated south of Gallup, New Mexico, where Zuñi Pueblo now stands. It was inhabited by the Zuñi people, members of a larger group whom the Spaniards came to call the Pueblos. When later generations of Spanish settlers came to the American Southwest, they found some Indians living in towns, while others were nomadic. The Spaniards called the sedentary people Pueblos (Spanish for towns), and the term remains in use.

In Coronado's time, as is true today, various Pueblo Indian communities dotted the land in northern Arizona and New Mexico. Cíbola, which had been Coronado's destination, was a region made up of six Pueblo villages. Each village (or pueblo) was about the size of Háwikuh. The people there owned a few gemstones, mainly turquoise. None of the Cíbolan pueblos was rich in gold or silver.

Surely Coronado felt as heartbroken as his men to discover the first city of Cíbola was a humble village instead of the magnificent metropolis he had hoped to see. But as commander, Coronado had duties to perform. First he had to secure food for his half-starved army. He knew the only food available in this wilderness must lie in the village storehouses. Spanish law also obliged him to read the *requerimiento* (requirement). The *requerimiento* was a formal document that all Spanish commanders read to newly discovered peoples in the Americas. It announced that the people were now subjects of the Spanish king and that they must become Christians. They had no choice but to comply. Resistance to the *requerimiento* was punishable by death.

As Coronado approached the walled town, two to three hundred village men formed ranks in front of the entrance. The men carried bows, arrows, and war clubs. Dutifully Coronado began to read the *requerimiento*. His words were translated by Indian guides the Spaniards had met before crossing the *despoblado*. Coronado's reading was interrupted by menacing shouts from the warriors. The shouts needed no translations: Get out of here, you white foreigners. Go back where you came from.

Experienced Indian fighters in the Spanish ranks were impressed by the Cíbolans' courage. These were a remote people. They had never before seen a white man, a gun, or—most important—a horse. Many warriors in Mexico panicked the first time they saw a man riding a horse. Some Mexican Indians believed the horse and the rider were one and the same being. The Cíbolans, on the other hand, seemed to regard the horse as a curious but not an otherworldly beast.

The buffalo, or American bison

They had all seen elk and buffalo. Also, they had little fear of enemies, since they lived undisturbed in their rugged land and felt themselves masters of their own domain.

As Coronado continued to read, the warriors fired a hail of arrows. Soldiers in the Spanish ranks begged their commander to order an attack. But Coronado was mindful of his instructions from Viceroy Mendoza and from the bishop of Mexico: If at all possible, the northland was to be conquered without bloodshed. More war cries resounded from the Cíbolan defenders. Another volley of arrows swished toward the Spanish soldiers. Finally even the priests urged an attack.

Coronado's attack on the walled town of Háwikuh

"*Santiago!*" Coronado cried. This was a sacred word, an appeal to St. James, the patron of the Spanish army. The commander then shouted the ancient Spanish war cry. "*Santiago, y a ellos!*"—"St. James, and at them!"

"*Santiago! Santiago!*" the soldiers hollered as they rushed the Cíbolan warriors.

Seven centuries of warfare in their homeland had turned the Spanish troops into fanatical fighting machines. No soldiers on earth could match their fury. The Cíbolans retreated behind their village walls. They outnumbered the Spaniards at least three to one. But never before had they faced such well-armed and determined enemy troops.

The battle lasted a little over an hour. Several Indians were killed. Significantly, this clash at Cíbola

East of Háwikuh stood the mountaintop village of Acoma, where lookouts could spot enemies from miles away. Residents of Acoma remained safe from attack by the Spaniards.

was the first combat to take place between Indians and Europeans in the American Southwest. Over the next 350 years, endless battles between the two groups were fought on Southwestern soil, and a nightmarish amount of blood was spilled.

At the gates of the village, the Spaniards suffered only one serious casualty. This occurred when their commander was hit by a storm of rocks and knocked unconscious. The Cíbolans were skilled warriors who knew they could weaken their enemy by killing its leader. Coronado, dressed in glittering armor, was clearly the chief, and Cíbolan defenders aimed their arrows and other missiles primarily at him. He might have been killed had his lieutenants not dragged his stunned body out of harm's way.

With the Cíbolan warriors driven into the country-side, the Spaniards and their Indian allies raided the village looking for food. Most of the men were near collapse from hunger. To their delight, they discovered an abundance of provisions in the pueblo storehouses. One member of the party wrote, "We found that of which there was a greater need than of gold and silver, which was corn, and beans, and fowl, better than those of New Spain." Eventually the Indian warriors driven off by the Spanish attack drifted back to the village. An uneasy peace prevailed.

Coronado lay unconscious for hours. When he finally recovered from his wounds he wrote a letter to the viceroy and sent it to Mexico City with a team of riders. "God knows that I wish I had better news to write," said Coronado, "but I must tell you the truth." Cíbola, Coronado confessed, was a major disappointment. There were no large cities in the region, and no evidence of gold.

Coronado also ordered Marcos de Niza to return to New Spain with the dispatch riders. The commander feared some disgruntled soldier would take the priest's life if he remained. Coronado's own disgust with Niza is clear in his note to the viceroy: "I can assure your Lordship that in reality, he [Niza] has not told the truth in a single thing that he has said, but everything is the reverse of what he has said."

Historians still argue why Marcos de Niza spun such wild stories about the land north of New Spain. Some claim that heat waves and the vastness of the desert put mirages in his mind, causing canyons to look like terraced cities. Others maintain Niza deliberately lied so he could claim some degree of fame, even though that fame would be short-lived. Still other historians hold that the priest was simply sloppy in writing his reports, relying upon rumors instead of facts. Whatever the reasons for the tall tales, Niza was forced to return in disgrace.

In the weeks after his initial contact with Háwikuh, Coronado visited the other towns in the Cíbola region. Pueblo runners spread the word of his coming. In a matter of days, all the villages in the land knew of these white-skinned intruders who fought with fire-sticks, rode on the backs of strange animals, and wore armor strong enough to ward off arrows. Neighboring communities welcomed Coronado, putting up no fight.

Pottery by Mary Small of New Mexico's Jemez Pueblo

Gradually the Spaniards learned the ways of the Pueblos. In many respects, the Pueblo people were the direct opposites of Europeans. Religion and art dominated their lives, and they cared little for material possessions. The Pueblos believed in a single, all-powerful creator and a host of lesser spirits and gods. In their parched land, the rain god was a mighty deity. Many tribal prayers were devoted to the rain god's pleasure. Prayers often took the form of passionate dances. Pueblo artists created items that were both practical and beautiful. Potters made lovely jars and bowls and painted them with symbols of the gods. Weavers fashioned straw baskets so tightly they could carry water without leaking a single drop.

The Pueblo people were the descendants of a great culture called the Anasazi (a Navajo word meaning "the ancient ones"). Beginning around A.D. 700, the Anasazi built great cities in the American Southwest. For unknown reasons, they abandoned their cities several hundred years before Coronado arrived. Now their descendants lived in smaller villages like those at Cíbola. Still, the people retained their building skills. Some of their houses towered seven stories high.

Hopi children, descendants of the Anasazi, performing traditional dances during a celebration at Second Mesa Day School

Orderly and well tended farms surrounded each village in Cíbola. Most of the farms employed some sort of irrigation system. The farmers grew corn, beans, squashes, and other vegetables. Theirs was not the sweet corn we eat today. The Pueblo people grew maize, a hard-kerneled corn, which they ground up to make the flat cakes that Mexicans call tortillas. "They make the best corn cakes I have seen anywhere," wrote Coronado, "and that is what everybody ordinarily eats. They have the very best arrangement and method for grinding [corn] that was ever seen. One of these Indian women here will grind as much flour as four of the Mexicans do."

Maize, squash, and beans grown in the traditional way at a pueblo in New Mexico

Pueblo women carrying water up the mountainside in jars

The Spaniards learned that the Pueblos waged war only in self-defense. One of the chiefs apologized to Coronado for the death of Estéban. The chief claimed the slave assaulted a village woman. Disturbing a woman in any manner was a serious crime in Pueblo society. The Spaniards learned to admire Pueblo morality. Castañeda wrote, "[The holy men] tell them how to live, and I believe they are given certain commandments for them to keep, for there is no drunkenness among them . . . nor sacrifices. . . . They are usually at work."

At Cíbola a dramatic transformation seemed to overcome Coronado. He had journeyed north from New Spain to find gold. But the disappointment of Cíbola dashed his hopes of discovering treasure in the lands north of New Spain. Putting dreams of riches aside, he began to think in the manner of a pure explorer. In his letter to the viceroy, Coronado said, "I have determined to send men throughout all the surrounding regions in order to find out whether there is anything,

A Pueblo city in the 1870s, with sheep pens below the town

and to suffer any extremity rather than give up this enterprise."

The Spaniards in the American Southwest then launched a remarkable period of exploration. In the months to come, exploration parties ventured out of Cíbola boldly plunging into the unknown. The men on those parties discovered some of the most spectacular natural wonders that could be found anywhere on earth.

García López de Cárdenas, one of Coronado's lieutenants, was the first European to see the wonders of the Grand Canyon in northern Arizona. Artist Edward Moran painted this view, called "Canyon Mists: Zoroaster Peak."

Chapter 6
The Summer of Discovery

"Accordingly, when they had marched for twenty days they came to the gorges of the river, from the edge it looked as if the opposite side was more than nine miles away."

—Pedro de Castañeda, describing the reactions of the first Europeans to see the Grand Canyon of the Colorado River

Coronado established a base camp at Cíbola. From this base he launched four major exploration missions during the summer of 1540. Coronado himself did not lead any of these exploring parties. The four missions were commanded by his most trusted lieutenants—Tovar, Cárdenas, Díaz, and Alvarado. These men carried the Spanish flag to lands ranging from modern-day New Mexico to California. In a single season of discovery, Coronado's men opened a vast new world to the dreams of future European pioneers.

The first of the history-making exploration parties left Cíbola in August 1540, led by Don Pedro de Tovar. Traveling in a northwesterly direction, Tovar's men hoped to find a region the Cíbolans called Tusayán. According to Cíbolan traders, the country of Tusayán was made up of seven villages. Just the thought of seven villages worked magic on the Spaniards. Could the seven towns of Tusayán be the Seven Golden Cities of legend? Although Coronado's dreams of finding treasure in this land had diminished, his officers and men still burned with gold fever.

The Tovar party soon entered a desert land where purple, gray, and rust-colored soils combined to paint a fantastic natural landscape. The desert received its technicolor appearance from rock sediments buried in the sand. The Spaniards also noticed that the desert's brilliant colors seemed to change hour by hour. At dawn a blue hue hung over the land, while at sunset a fiery red color dominated. Later Spanish settlers called this region the *Desierto Pintado*, or Painted Desert. It is now the Painted Desert National Monument, situated just north of the Petrified Forest in northeast Arizona.

After about 75 miles (194 kilometers) of rugged traveling, Tovar saw a settlement made up of terraced houses. From a distance some Spaniards thought it was a great city. But once more, disappointment swept the ranks as the first settlement of Tusayán proved to be much the same as the villages of Cíbola.

Tusayán was home to a remarkable Pueblo group called the Hopi. People of the Hopi culture had inhabited the land for at least five hundred years before Coronado's journey. Holy men who recited Hopi legends were the most revered individuals in their community. One Hopi legend held that four races—black, white, yellow, and red—lived on the earth. The origin of this legend is unknown, since the Hopi had never left their isolated region, where only the "red" race lived. Still, they were not surprised when traders told them that white strangers had arrived at neighboring Cíbola. Now, as Tovar's men approached, they looked upon the whites as they would upon any potential enemy.

Tovar marched forward to find a group of Hopi warriors guarding the entrance of the village. Some of

The Painted Desert

the warriors had made a line in the sand with their sacred cornmeal. The meaning of the line was clear to the Spaniards—crossing it meant war. Dutifully Tovar read the *requerimiento* to the Hopi. Tovar's unit consisted of seventeen horsemen and a few foot soldiers. They faced at least two hundred Hopi. One Hopi youth rushed a Spaniard's horse and tried to club the animal.

"*Santiago, y a ellos!*" Tovar shouted.

"*Santiago! Santiago!*" echoed his men as they attacked the Hopi ranks. After just minutes of fighting, the Hopi leaders made gestures asking for peace.

The Hopi village of Walpi, atop First Mesa, was in the region known as Tusayán. Walpi was built shortly after the Pueblo Revolt of 1680 against the Spaniards.

Tovar visited Tusayán and neighboring villages. Wherever he traveled, the people showered the Spaniards with gifts, including pieces of turquoise, beautifully woven robes, and cakes made of ground-up pine nuts. The Hopi had no gold or silver, but they did have important information. They told Tovar of a great river to the west of their community. Tovar returned to Cíbola and gave his commander a complete report.

Hearing about the river led Coronado to order a second mission of discovery. Perhaps this river was the waterway to the Pacific, for which Europeans had been searching since Columbus's first voyage. If the river did indeed lead to the Pacific, Coronado's men could link up with three Spanish ships that were at this time sailing along the Pacific coast. The ships

Ruins of the village of Awatovi on Antelope Mesa in the Tusayán region. The town was inhabited during Coronado's time.

were commanded by Captain Hernando de Alarcón, whose orders were twofold: first, he was to draw maps of the Pacific coastline north of Mexico; second, he was to meet and deliver food and equipment to Coronado's army

* * * * *

In late August 1540, a unit made up of a dozen horsemen rode out of the camp at Cíbola. The party was commanded by Don García López de Cárdenas, who would later play a foul role in the Coronado drama. Retracing Tovar's trail, Cárdenas first rode to Tusayán. There he was well received and given food and guides. For twenty days Cárdenas traveled west over difficult mountain terrain. Finally he arrived at one of the world's greatest natural wonders.

Below Cárdenas spread the Grand Canyon of the Colorado River. Countless centuries of rushing water had carved this magnificent gash in the earth, sculpting it into the breathtaking monument we hail today. Historians believe the Spaniards approached the canyon edge near Grandview, a popular spot for modern tourists to gather.

Cárdenas later wrote an official report containing his impressions of the canyon, but that report has been lost. The only account we have of the first Europeans to visit the Grand Canyon comes from Pedro de Castañeda, who was not with the party. Castañeda recorded the descriptions he heard from returning soldiers. It seemed that none of the men commented on the canyon's profound beauty. In fact, they complained the area was inhospitable. Castañeda wrote, "This region was high and covered with low and twisting pine trees; it was extremely cold, being open to the north, so that, although this was the warm season, no one could live in this canyon because of the cold."

For three days Cárdenas and his troops scouted along the canyon's rim, looking for a way to climb down to the river. Finally Cárdenas found a spot where the descent seemed less difficult, and he sent three of his "most agile" men down the canyon walls. All day the three descended, clinging to the cliffs. According to Castañeda, the three men "returned about four o'clock in the afternoon, as they could not reach the bottom because of the many obstacles they met, for what from the top seemed easy was not so; on the contrary, it was rough and difficult."

The Grand Canyon is a mile (1.6 kilometer) deep and anywhere from 10 to 15 miles (10 to 24 kilometers) wide. So vast is this natural ditch that its dimensions confound the eyes. What appears to be a relatively easy descent into the canyon proves to be an exhausting trek that lasts several days. Cárdenas's men, the best climbers in the group, managed to go only about one-third of the way down the canyon's rugged walls.

At this point, the Cárdenas party was running desperately short of water. This shortage was an incredible irony, because below them gushed the broad Colorado River. The steep canyon walls, however, made the Colorado as unreachable as the face of the moon. Cárdenas had no choice but to return to Cíbola. He had seen the Grand Canyon in all its raw glory, untouched by civilization, yet his report to Coronado was gloomy. The great canyon had prevented him from completing his mission to follow the Colorado to its mouth.

View of the Grand Canyon from Mather Point

Of all the expeditions undertaken by Coronado's lieutenants during the summer of discovery, none blazed more new trails or covered more ground than that headed by Melchor Díaz. Unlike Coronado's other officers, Melchor Díaz was not born into a noble family. He was a peasant who had won the respect of the gentleman class. As an experienced scout, no man in New Spain knew more about the northern frontier and its people than did Melchor Díaz.

Coronado instructed Díaz to head south and join the main army at its base camp in northern Mexico. Once he located the army, he was to send the major forces north to Cíbola. A smaller unit was to remain in the base camp while Díaz took a group of soldiers

This map shows the exploration routes of Coronado and the men he sent out. Melchor Díaz's route is the one that follows the Gulf of California and crosses the Colorado River into California.

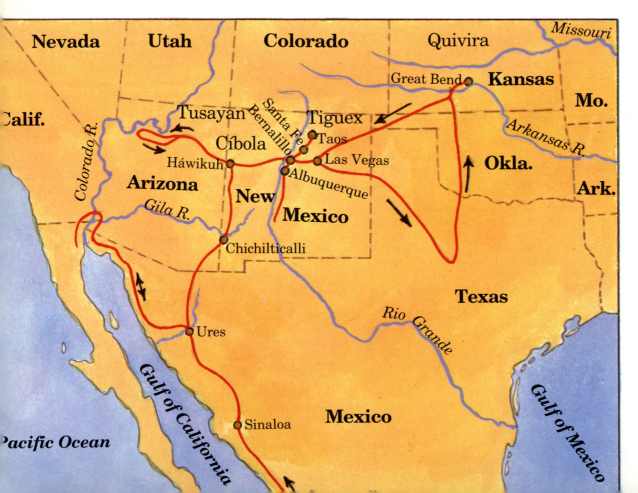

Present-day view along Camino del Diablo in southwest Arizona

west to the sea. Coronado hoped Melchor Díaz would link up with the three ships prowling the coastline laden with much-needed supplies.

After completing a long journey south, Melchor Díaz found the army camped along the Sonora River just south of the present-day border between Mexico and Arizona. Obeying his instructions, he took twenty-five Spanish soldiers and a contingent of Indian allies and marched west. His journey proceeded over a life-less desert. So desolate was his route that later groups of Spaniards called the path he had chosen *Camino del Diablo*—the Devil's Highway. Even today, a luck-less traveler whose car breaks down on an isolated road in the northwestern Mexican state of Sonora can die of thirst or exposure to the brutal sun.

An exhausting 300-mile (483-kilometer) hike led Melchor Díaz and his men to the banks of a broad river. This was the Colorado, the same river that farther north carved out the Grand Canyon. The men encountered the riverbank about 60 miles (97 kilometers) upstream from its mouth at the Gulf of California.

In the river country the Spaniards met the Yuma Indians. Upon first sight they called the Yumas "giants" because of their great height and bulging muscles. "When transporting burdens [these giants] carried on their heads more than three or four hundred pounds," wrote Castañeda. "It once happened that when our men wished to bring a log and six of them were unable to carry it, one of the Yuma Indians

The Colorado River where it forms the Arizona-California border

picked it up in his arms, put it on his head all by himself, and carried it with great ease."

Melchor Díaz was so astounded at the size and bear-like strength of the Yumas that he wanted to capture one and show him to Viceroy Mendoza in Mexico City. Spotting a young man alone, a group of Spaniards attempted to overpower the youth and tie him up. Castañeda reports the attempt at capture was a colossal failure: "[The young man] made such a resistance that four Spaniards were unable to bind him." It is no wonder that descendants of the Yuma people in northern Mexico and southern Arizona later became outstanding athletes, excelling in wrestling and football.

From the Yumas, Melchor Díaz learned that three large ships had sailed up the Colorado River some weeks earlier. Díaz marched downriver until he found a huge tree with a message carved on its trunk: ALARCÓN CAME THIS FAR. THERE ARE LETTERS AT THE FOOT OF THIS TREE. Díaz dug up the letters, which were written by Captain Alarcón. They said he had waited for the overland party as long as possible. Finally he was forced to sail to his home port because the wooden beams of his ships were rotting.

Although Díaz and Alarcón failed to link up, their two missions added to Spanish knowledge of the Gulf of California. Alarcón determined that the land and waters there formed a gulf instead of open sea as previously thought. Also, reports of the two missions helped mapmakers to realize the region they called California was part of the American mainland. Some mapmakers of the time believed that what is now the state of California was an island isolated in the Pacific Ocean.

Marching north along the Colorado River, Melchor Díaz fought a brief but bloody battle with the Yumas. He then crossed the Colorado and headed west. Upon fording the river, he became the first European to enter California by the overland route. California held a fearful welcome for the Spanish travelers. "While they were traveling," reported Castañeda, "they came upon some beds of burning lava. No one could cross them, for it would be like going into the sea to drown. It was amazing to see the cinders boil, for it looked like something infernal. They turned away from this place because it seemed so dangerous." They were near southern California's Imperial Valley, where mud volcanoes and hot springs still bubble out of the ground. The Spaniards believed it to be the home of the devil.

The Melchor Díaz expedition ended in tragedy for its leader. In a fit of fury, Melchor Díaz hurled a lance at the expedition's dog. The lance stuck in the sand, and while riding at full speed, the Spaniard rammed into the butt end of the weapon. He died several days later of internal injuries. Melchor Díaz is buried somewhere in the desert country of southern California. His grave has never been found.

* * * * *

A fourth mission of discovery launched that summer was led by Don Hernando de Alvarado, a favorite lieutenant of Coronado. Alvarado was given twenty men and sent to explore to the east. Indian traders told Coronado that grasslands to the east nurtured the strange beasts the Spaniards called cows. No European had ever before seen the American bison.

Alvarado's guide was a handsome, talkative Indian who had wandered into the white men's camp. He lived in the east and was eager to return home.

Inscription House, an Anasazi site in Arizona's Navajo National Monument, shows how the Anasazi made homes in the sides of cliffs.

The Spaniards nicknamed him Bigotes, Spanish for mustache. Facial hair was rare among Indians, but Bigotes had long, flowing whiskers.

Heading out of Cíbola, the Spaniards under Alvarado gazed at the ruins of ancient villages. Some were primitive cliff dwellings; others were long-abandoned cities. These were the remaining monuments of the Anasazi civilization, which had risen to greatness and then suddenly and mysteriously declined. Alvarado wrote, "We came to an old edifice resembling a fortress; a league farther on we found another one, and a little father on, still another."

Lava field near Grants, New Mexico

South of present-day Grants, New Mexico, Alvarado trekked across ground that some of his men must have thought to be the floor of hell. Five centuries earlier a volcano had erupted, covering this region with a thick coating of lava. The lava hardened into what looked like a frozen ocean, rippling with black waves of rock. For men and horses alike, the hike over this terrain was agony.

Beyond the lava field the Spaniards beheld the incredible pueblo of Acoma. Called the "Sky City," Acoma astonishes visitors even today. It is a village built on the peak of a flat-topped mountain rising as

Stairs carved into sandstone cliffs lead up to the "Sky City" of Acoma Pueblo in New Mexico.

high as a ten-story office building. In Alvarado's time, its residents went to and from their city by climbing stairways that had been chiseled into the sides of sheer cliffs. No one knows exactly when the Sky City was built. Historians now believe Acoma may be the oldest continuously occupied site in the United States. The Spaniards were greatly relieved when the men of Acoma greeted them as friends. Attacking the town would have been impossible for Alvarado's small band. One member of the party claimed that Acoma, perched on a mountaintop, was "the greatest stronghold ever seen in the world."

Bigotes next led the Spaniards to a fertile valley carved out by the Rio Grande River. The Rio Grande flows through the heart of present-day New Mexico and then loops southeastward to become the borderline between the United States and Mexico. Alvarado's men reached the Upper Rio Grande at a point just north of present-day Albuquerque.

As they traveled along the riverbanks, Alvarado was surprised by the richness of the valley lands. It was harvest time, and the fields farmed by Pueblo groups burst forth with corn, beans, and squashes. Indian guides told Alvarado the country supported at least sixty settlements. Alvarado wrote, "The natives here seem to be good people, more devoted to agriculture than war." The Spaniards called this fruitful river land Tiguex, a corruption of the Indian word Tigua. After spending several days in the region, Alvarado dispatched a letter to Coronado, urging him to move the army to Tiguex and establish a winter camp there.

Beyond Tiguex, the mustached guide Bigotes led Alvarado to his home village called Cicúye. The villagers welcomed the Spaniards with musicians who played fifes and drums. Bigotes, the Spaniards found out, was a popular village chief. But it was at Cicúye that the explorers met an Indian slave who once was a member of a tribe that lived far to the east. The Spaniards called this slave the Turk, because "he looked like one." The Turk would later have a profound influence on the Coronado mission.

Alvarado traveled far east of Tiguex to find the flatlands that held the miraculous "cows." Soon he and his men were confronted with herds of bison so thick they darkened the grasslands. On the run, their hoofbeats sounded like thunder. One of Alvarado's men wrote, "Within four days we came upon the cows, which are the most monstrous beasts ever seen or read about. . . . There are such multitudes of them that I do not know what to compare them with unless it be the fish in the sea."

What Alvarado's men saw was an example of American wildlife in all its unspoiled splendor. In those days an estimated sixty million bison lived on the Great Plains. People today will never know the thrill of seeing huge buffalo herds racing over the grasslands like great black clouds.

Millions of bison, now scarce, once roamed the Great Plains.

Chapter 7
A Winter of War

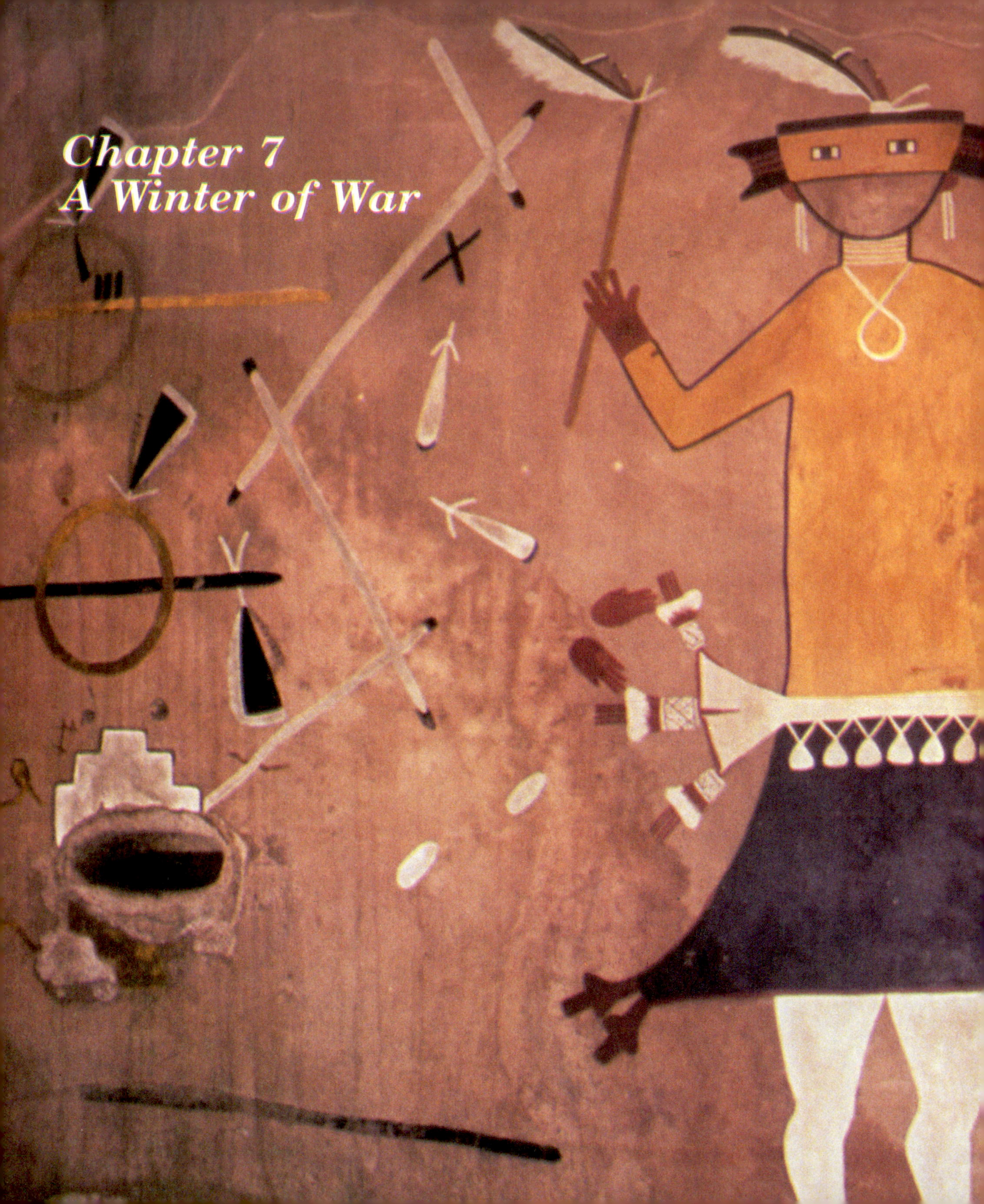

"While [the Pueblos and the Spaniards] were at peace, without any legitimate cause, the general [Coronado] and his captains, set dogs on the chiefs. . . . He set dogs on them so that they should bite them, and they did bite them. . . . So the province turned from peace to war and remained at war. As a result the natives killed many Spaniards, and the whole army was in danger. And because of it all, many of the natives were burned alive and put to the sword."

—*Charges brought against Coronado by a Spanish court several years after the mission was completed*

Alvarado's report from Tiguex intrigued Coronado. The land surrounding his camp at Cíbola was parched. He had already ordered the main force of his army—including many sheep and pack animals—to march north and join him. But Cíbola had insufficient water for the additional animals and men. Coronado decided to establish his winter camp in Tiguex country on the banks of the Rio Grande.

Before Coronado arrived at Tiguex, an interesting and fateful drama unfolded. While on a routine expedition, the slave nicknamed the Turk told Lieutenant Hernando de Alvarado that his home far to the east overflowed with gold. So much precious metal lay in the soil that, according to the Turk, the Spaniards would need wagons to haul it away. The country the Turk extolled was called Quivira. Once again the Spaniards seized upon the magic of a name. In their fantasies, Quivira became the legendary home of the wandering bishops, where gold was as common as sand.

Alvarado, though caught up in gold giddiness, demanded to see some form of evidence. If gold was so plentiful in Quivira, then why was the Turk not wearing a gold object of some kind? The Turk said he once owned a fine gold bracelet. The bracelet was taken from him when he was captured and enslaved by the people of Cicúye. Chief Bigotes of Cicúye now kept the bracelet in a special hiding place. Alvarado, anxious to see the golden bracelet, hurried to Cicúye.

Thus far, Coronado's forces had managed to avoid prolonged and bloody war with the Indians. As an obedient public servant, Coronado had complied with the orders of the Mexican bishop that the conquest of the lands to the north be "Christian and not a butchery." But as snow began to fall over the Upper Rio

New Mexico's Taos Pueblo, north of Pecos (Cicúye), reflects the Pueblo peoples' centuries-old building skills.

Grande, the peace between the Europeans and the Pueblo people dissolved. The atrocities committed by Coronado and his officers during the winter of war, 1540 to 1541, forever condemned the mission as a dark and brutal chapter in the pages of history.

At Cicúye, Alvarado confronted the mustached chief Bigotes. Where, he demanded, was the bracelet taken from the Turk? Bigotes told him the slave was a liar, and that no such bracelet ever existed. According to some reports, Alvarado's men then unleashed several of their huge dogs and encouraged the animals to attack and bite the chief. Still, Bigotes held firm that the slave wore no bracelet when he was captured. Alvarado responded by putting the chief in chains and dragging him from the village.

Spaniards used vicious war dogs against Indians of the New World.

Lieutenant Alvarado's actions were treacherous as well as ironic: treacherous, because Alvarado and Chief Bigotes became good friends during the weeks they traveled together from Cíbola; ironic, because Bigotes served as a peacemaker as well as a guide while leading the Spaniards. Along the trail, Bigotes had persuaded many Pueblo villagers to greet the Spaniards in peace instead of by waging war. Now Alvarado threatened that peace by arresting the peacemaker.

Another of Coronado's lieutenants, García López de Cárdenas, also fed the fires of friction between Spaniards and Pueblos. Seeking winter quarters, Cárdenas entered a Tiguex village and demanded that the residents leave. Too stunned by his brashness to resist, the villagers gave up their houses, taking with them only the clothes on their backs. Cárdenas and his soldiers moved into the houses and seized the food the village people had stored for the winter. Meanwhile, the winter season descended with unusual fury. Spanish reports say the snow piled as high as the horses' shoulders.

The people of Tiguex were near rebellion when Coronado arrived. But instead of defusing the situation, the Spanish commander inflamed it. Deciding his men were poorly clothed, Coronado went from pueblo to pueblo, confiscating blankets and winter coats. Even the foot soldier Castañeda was struck by Coronado's unfairness. He wrote: "These people could do nothing but take off their own cloaks and donate them. . . . And [when] some of [our] soldiers . . . saw an Indian with a better coat on, they exchanged with him without more ado, not stopping to find out the rank of the man they were stripping, which caused not a little hard feeling."

Nineteenth-century drawing of a Pueblo Indian

The final spark that touched off the winter of war came when a Spanish soldier assaulted an Indian woman. Coronado understood the high place women held among the Pueblos, and he moved to punish the Spaniard. Assembling a field court, Coronado summoned the husband of the woman who had suffered the assault. The man had witnessed the attack but said he could not point out the guilty Spanish soldier because to him all white men looked alike. He could, however, identify the Spaniard's horse. Coronado ruled that it was impossible to pronounce a Spaniard guilty of an offense because a witness identified his horse. The case was dropped, leaving the Pueblo men furious.

Winter in the Sangre de Cristo Mountains in northern New Mexico, near where Coronado and his men spent the winter of 1540-41

The winter war began the day after Coronado dismissed charges in the assault case. Seeking revenge, a band of Pueblo men attacked a Spanish corral and made off with thirty horses and mules. Coronado assigned Lieutenant Cárdenas to launch a retaliatory raid on an Indian village. The horror that followed shocked even Spanish authorities who reviewed the case years later.

Storming the village with muskets and crossbows, Cárdenas drove the defenders into the central kiva, the village place of worship. A dugout structure with a low roof, the kiva was the most sacred place in Pueblo society. Perhaps the retreating warriors believed the gods of their kiva would protect them from the Spaniards. If so, they were wrong. The Spaniards and their Indian allies threw burning branches into

"Coronado at Pecos," a painting by artist Roy Andersen. Pecos is the site of the Pueblo town of Cicúye.

the kiva's opening, and the Indians were smoked out like wasps from a nest. As the choking men staggered outside, they were easily captured. Cárdenas held about two hundred Pueblo warriors as prisoners.

Sentence was swift. For stealing Spanish horses, Cárdenas ordered all two hundred Pueblo men to be tied to stakes and burned to death. At first the Indian prisoners had no idea what cruel fate awaited them. They stared dumbfounded as Spaniards drove large poles in the ground and piled sticks and logs at their bases. Then several of the captives were pulled forward, tied to stakes, and the fires were lit. Screams and the horrible smell of burning flesh filled the air. The remaining captives panicked as they realized they had the choice between two deaths—either to be burned slowly or to die fighting.

The remains of an underground kiva at the Cliff Palace site in Mesa Verde National Park, Colorado

Artist Peter Hurd's charcoal drawing of Coronado, with a yucca plant and a destroyed pueblo in the background

Breaking away from their guards, the Indians picked up stones and sticks and flung them at the Spaniards. When recaptured, they fought back with their hands and feet, their fingernails, and their teeth. But they had no chance. All two hundred warriors were killed. Spanish records do not say the number who died by the sword or the number of those who suffered the agony of the stake. The massacre was one of the most cold-blooded acts of mass murder ever committed in what is now the southwestern United States.

Coronado's men also stormed other Tiguex villages, forcing the residents out of their homes and leaving

Anasazi cliff dwellings, high on a hillside in Bandelier National Monument, New Mexico. Indians occupied this site until around the year 1550.

burned and destroyed buildings in their wake. Tiguex warriors retreated to the pueblo of Moho, the best constructed of their towns. There, behind high walls, they determined to make a final stand against the foreign invaders.

In January 1541, Coronado surrounded Moho pueblo. Trudging over the icy ground, the Spanish commander approached the village wall. He read the *requerimiento* and urged the warriors to abandon their village. His words were greeted with jeers. Coronado reacted in the tradition of the Spanish army: "*Santiago, y a ellos!*"

Screaming *"Santiago! Santiago!"* the soldiers rushed the city. They carried ladders to scale Moho's walls. But from the top of the walls, Indian defenders fired arrows and hurled rocks down on the heads of the attackers. The battle was reminiscent of the medieval era when armies commanded by feudal lords stormed an opponent's castle.

The first assault on Moho failed as the Spaniards were driven off by an avalanche of arrows and boulders. Thus began a siege that lasted almost two months. Periodically the Spaniards attacked, only to be beaten back by the Pueblo men perched on the city's walls. The frustrated Spaniards resorted to novel methods of assault. One of them wrote, "[We built] some engines with timbers, which the men called swings, like the old rams with which they battered fortresses in the times before gunpowder was invented; but they did no good. Then, lacking artillery, [we] attempted to make some wooden tubes tightly bound with cords, on the order of rockets; but these did not serve either."

As the winter weeks dragged on, it became clear that time was on Coronado's side. The Indians defending Moho had precious little water. They tried to dig a well, but instead of striking water the well collapsed, burying thirty of the diggers. Finally a heavy snow fell, covering the pueblo and giving its residents a temporary water supply. When the snow melted, however, Coronado and his soldiers remained ringing the walls, poised to attack.

In mid-March 1541, the defenders of Moho called for a truce. With the assistance of interpreters, they asked if the women and children within the walled town could be released and come to no harm at the

At Pecos National Monument in New Mexico stand the ruins of this mission church built in the 1700s.

hands of the Spaniards. Coronado agreed, and when the women and children streamed out of Moho they were given food and water. The siege continued until the desperate men tried to sneak out of the city under cover of night. They were discovered and hacked to death by Spanish swordsmen.

The collapse of Moho marked the end of the winter war of 1540-41. The people of Tiguex now recognized Coronado as their conqueror. But hatred toward the Spaniard and his men seethed in their hearts.

Chapter 8
The Promise of Quivira

"They do not live in houses, but have some sets of poles which they carry with them to erect huts at places where they stop. . . . They tie these poles together at the top and stick the bottoms into the ground, covering them with buffalo skins."

—*Juan Jaramillo, one of Coronado's officers, describing houses used by the Plains Indians*

Peace in the land of Tiguex came with the arrival of spring. The snow melted into mud and the Rio Grande broke up into chunks. Spring breezes gave Coronado and his men the urge to move on again in search of new lands. So far the mission had been a dismal failure. Though they had seen much, they made the long journey in hopes of finding gold. The officers and men still clung to the belief that somewhere in this unknown land stood cities rich in treasure.

All winter the men's fantasies were excited by tales told them by the slave nicknamed the Turk. As the army shivered in the snow, his stories grew even wilder. Not only was his home city of Quivira rich, but beyond it were cities named Arache and Guas, whose wealth made Quivira seem impoverished by comparison. The Turk had no evidence of the treasures to be found in his homeland, but the troops believed what they wanted to believe. Giving in to the wishes of his men, Coronado launched a new expedition late in April 1541. This time the Spaniards trekked east, toward the city of Quivira.

For this new mission, Coronado's ranks had swelled. His main force, including hundreds of Indian allies, had joined him from northern Mexico. The herds of sheep, mules, and pack horses had also been moved to Tiguex, and now many of these animals joined in the big push east.

Beyond the Pecos River, Coronado's army entered the buffalo country that Alvarado had seen earlier. North American wildlife fascinated Coronado. In a letter to the viceroy he described the incredible assortment of animals he had seen: "There are many animals, bears, mountain lions, porcupines, and sheep as big as horses." But nothing prepared the commander for his first sight of the buffalo. Great shifting herds of bison spread from horizon to horizon. The army had entered the southern end of the Great Plains, America's vast sea of grass. This land supported what was perhaps the greatest concentration of four-legged animals in the world. "There was not a day that I lost sight of [the buffaloes]," Coronado wrote.

Coronado's men began calling the great beasts *vacas de Cíbola* or "cows of Cíbola." Later the words were shortened to *cibolo*, which is still one of the Spanish names for the American bison. So immense were the Great Plains buffalo herds that they supported satellite packs of gray wolves that milled about the herd's flanks, pulling down calves or weak adults. Countless deer grazed alongside the buffaloes. Swift pronghorn antelopes darted through the tall grasses. The Spaniards were surprised by the large jackrabbits that hopped boldly in front of their horses. At that time, the rabbits were unable to sense a man riding a horse as an enemy, and they were easily speared by Spanish hunters.

Northern white-tailed deer of the North American Great Plains

The Great Plains itself mystified the Spaniards. Never before had they seen such an immense flatland so totally devoid of hills, mountains, or even a grove of trees. They could not have guessed that this amazing stretch of level ground spread northward, far beyond what is now the Canadian border. Hundreds of years later, American settlers called the Great Plains the prairie. The Spaniards had another name for the endless open country—the *Llano Estacado* or "staked plains." They believed a traveler in this region had to drive stakes into the ground to serve as landmarks, or risk becoming hopelessly lost.

Spaniards traveling on the Great Plains were struck by scenes such as this one, where prairie land stretches toward the horizon in all directions.

Castañeda compared his surroundings to "the inside of a bowl, so that wherever a man stands the sky hems him in." To assist stragglers and lost hunting parties, Coronado ordered his men to fire their muskets at regular intervals, and to build fires of buffalo dung at night. Still, the expedition lost several soldiers who died of thirst or exposure while wandering in circles wildly looking for their camp.

On the endless ocean of grass, the Spaniards met Indian tribes whose life-styles were a world apart from those of the Pueblo people. The Plains Indians were nomadic buffalo hunters. They built no permanent homes and did not cultivate crops. Instead, the nomads followed the wanderings of the buffalo herds and lived entirely off the animals. A priest traveling with the Coronado party wrote: "With the skins they make their houses, with the skins they clothe and

Indians, disguised as wolves, hunting buffalo

shoe themselves, of the skins they make rope, and also of the wool; from the sinews they make thread, with which they sew their clothes and their houses; from the bones they make awls; the dung serves them for wood, the stomachs serve them for pitchers and vessels; they live on the flesh."

An unbalanced diet consisting of little else but buffalo meat led the Plains Indians to practice bizarre eating habits. Their meat-laden meals caused their bodies to cry out for vegetables and vegetable juices. They satisfied their cravings by cutting open the stomach of a freshly killed buffalo and drinking the juices they found inside. The juices contained partially digested grasses and made up practically the only vegetable material consumed by the Plains people. They considered the juices to be most tasty when drunk still warm from the animal's gut.

An Indian woman curing a buffalo hide to be used as a robe

In this drawing, an Apache holds out a deer's liver to capture a rattlesnake. Snakes' venom was used to poison arrow tips.

The first band of Plains Indians the Spaniards met were called the Querechos. Being buffalo hunters, the Querechos were animal-oriented. No doubt they looked at Spanish horses, which bore men so effortlessly, with a touch of wonder. Perhaps a good-natured Spanish soldier allowed a Querecho to ride on his horse. And perhaps the Indian was so thrilled by his experience that he told his children about it, and they told their children. It would seem that some kinship between Querechos and horses must have been established, because hundreds of years later the tribesmen became among the greatest horse soldiers ever known. Their name had changed—to the Apaches, the most feared riders and warriors of the American West.

Coronado continued his search for Quivira even though the flatness of the land confused him. "I trav-

A herd of buffalo enjoying the cool water of a river

eled as the guides wished to lead me, [over] plains with no more landmarks than as if we had been swallowed up by the sea . . . not a stone, nor a bit of rising ground, nor a tree, nor a shrub, or anything to go by." Every day the commander sent out scouting parties to probe ahead of the main army. Every day they returned and reported they saw nothing but "buffaloes and sky."

Also confusing were the directions given to Coronado by the Turk, his principal guide. The Turk led the Spaniards in a meandering fashion, drifting south as well as east. The Pueblo guides from Tiguex warned Coronado not to follow the directions of the slave, as he was a slippery character. But the wealth of Quivira played on Spanish dreams and Coronado mindlessly obeyed the slave's instructions.

After arriving in what is now the Texas panhandle, a host of troubles plagued the men. First the soldiers fought among themselves over a pile of buffalo skins given them by friendly Indians. Next the foreigners endured one of the treacherous weather shifts common in the area. "A violent whirlwind arose one afternoon," wrote Castañeda. "It began to hail and in a short time the hailstones fell . . . as thick as raindrops." The hailstones that pelted the men were the size of their fists. Many of the horses were injured.

On the plains Coronado's army met another band of nomadic buffalo hunters, this tribe called the Teyas. Castañeda said these rootless people were "very intelligent." Their tribal name—Teyas—later became the name of America's second largest state. The Teyas used domesticated wolves to help them move supplies over the grassland. They hitched harnesses to the wolves and the animals dragged loads of sticks that served as tent poles. Castañeda wrote, "When the load gets disarranged, the dogs howl, calling someone to straighten it out."

The trek over the featureless land seemed to be getting the Spaniards nowhere. At the beginning of the journey Coronado gave one of his foot soldiers the mind-numbing task of counting his steps so the commander could estimate the distance traveled. The man faithfully carried out the order, and each night told Coronado how many steps he had taken. Calculating distance by the number of steps, Coronado reasoned he should have been in Quivira long ago. Also, his guides from Tiguex claimed that Quivira was in a more northerly direction. They added that Quivira was little more than a village, and not a resplendent city, as the Turk claimed.

Summer storm over the Texas panhandle east of Canyon, Texas

In late May 1541, Coronado determined the progress of his large force was much too slow. He sent the main army back to Tiguex while he took a party of thirty horsemen and a dozen foot soldiers on a northerly course toward Quivira. This time Coronado followed the directions given him by the Pueblo guides he had brought from Tiguex. He took the Turk with him but ordered that the slave be brought in chains.

Coronado's small unit traveled north up the Texas panhandle and across Oklahoma's long, narrow stem. They entered what is now the state of Kansas near the present-day town of Ashland. The Spaniards thus became the first Europeans to visit the midwestern United States.

After a long hike through dry grasses, Coronado's men reached the banks of the Arkansas River, which flows through southern Kansas. The river brought great relief to Coronado and his soldiers, because water was scarce to the south. In a letter to King Charles, Coronado complained, "Many times I drank [water] which was so bad it tasted more like slime."

Along the Arkansas River Coronado encountered a group of Indians who were buffalo hunting. They claimed they were from Quivira. Coronado asked them to describe their land. Quivira, they said, was a collection of villages. And gold? There was no gold, said the Indians. No gold at all.

Coronado summoned the Turk and demanded to know why he had lied about the riches of Quivira. Some accounts say the Turk was tortured to get out

This straw lodge of the Wichita Indians is similar to the homes of the Quivirans in Coronado's time.

the truth. Finally the slave confessed he had made up the stories to trick the Spaniards into taking him home. Then he had guided the Spaniards on a southerly course as part of a conspiracy with the mustached chief Bigotes. The chief hated the Spaniards for imprisoning him and waging war on his people. Bigotes urged the Turk to lead the Europeans astray in hopes of weakening their horses. The mustached chief reasoned that if the horses were exhausted or dead, the Spaniards would be an easy enemy to defeat.

Coronado accepted the Turk's confession with little emotion. His dreams of finding treasure in this country had faded months ago. And perhaps he thought the wild goose chase to Quivira was God's punishment for his own people's greed.

Coronado's march through Kansas, by Kansas artist Albert T. Reid

A view south of Great Bend, Kansas, Coronado's "Quivira"

During the age of exploration, the Spanish lust for gold made them easy prey for crafty Indians. The conquistadores were brutes and the Indian people hoped they would leave their region, the sooner the better. Countless Indian leaders, aware of Spanish gold fever, told the Europeans that there was plenty of gold beyond the mountains many miles from their villages. Hearing this, the Spaniards hurried off, constantly seeking the end of the rainbow. The Indians rejoiced in their leaving.

Still wanting to see Quivira, Coronado and a small band of men followed the Arkansas River northwest. The land was pleasant, with trees hugging the riverbanks and streams winding through the tall grasses. Once they reached what is now the town of

A spring at the headwaters of the Little Arkansas River near Lyons, Kansas, between Great Bend and the Smoky Hill River

Great Bend, Kansas, the men trekked overland until they arrived at the banks of the Smoky Hill River. There they discovered several villages of Wichita Indians. The people were friendly but primitive. Along the trail the Spaniards were greeted by dogs and naked children.

Finally the party reached Quivira, a riverside village situated just west of present-day Abilene, Kansas. Even though the Turk had confessed his lies about Quivira's wealth, the sight of the village was a shock. Quivira was made up of squat grass huts looking like beehives lined up along the riverbank. Coronado expressed his bitterness in a letter to the king: "The people [of Quivira] are savage. . . . They have no blankets or cotton. . . . They eat raw meat."

Despite their disappointment, the Spaniards were impressed with the well watered and fertile land they saw spreading around them. After beholding the rich grasslands, Captain Juan Jaramillo wrote: "This country has a fine appearance, the like of which I have never seen anywhere in our Spain, Italy, or parts of France, nor indeed in other lands where I have traveled in service of his Majesty. It is not a hilly country, but one with mesas, plains, and charming rivers with fine waters. . . . I am of the belief that it will be very productive for all sorts of commodities."

The Spanish captain was correct in his prediction. Today this section of Kansas lies in the heart of the American Wheat Belt, whose farms feed millions of people all over the world.

Coronado remained in the Quivira region for almost a month. He sent scouting parties in all directions, but they found nothing of importance to the Spaniards. One scouting party may have traveled as far north as Nebraska. If so, those scouts marked the high-water mark of the Coronado expedition. Starting in Mexico City, the men had marched almost 3,000 miles (4,828 kilometers) north over unexplored and often forbidding terrain.

As the weeks passed, Coronado noticed a growing hostility among the Quivirans. He soon discovered that the Turk was secretly telling the people that the Spaniards were evil spirits. Furthermore, the slave urged the Quivirans to rise up and kill their unwanted guests. Coronado decided to deal firmly with his ex-guide. One of the men described his fate. "A soldier named Perez came from behind, put a rope around the Turk's neck, twisted it with a garrote, and choked him to death."

Fearing a winter on the open plains, Coronado decided to march his small unit back to Tiguex and join the main army. The party left Quivira in late August 1541. This time they took a direct route to the Rio Grande Valley instead of the winding course dictated by the Turk. The Indian path over which they traveled later became one of the most celebrated ways of passage in the history of the American West. It was called the Santa Fe Trail.

The Santa Fe Trail region near Las Vegas, New Mexico

Chapter 9
The Long Road Home

"Now when General Coronado saw that all was calm and that his plans had turned out according to his desires, he ordered everyone to be ready to start the return to New Spain in the early part of April, 1542."

—*Pedro de Castañeda*

The people of Tiguex and the nearby cities extended an icy welcome to the returning Spaniards. Painful memories of the winter of war remained with them. The town of Cicúye, home of Chief Bigotes, refused to allow the Spaniards to enter its walls. Only after weeks of persuasion did the people open their doors to the Europeans.

The second winter passed quietly for the Spaniards and their Pueblo neighbors on the Upper Rio Grande. By this time, dispatch runners were running regular routes between Tiguex and Coronado's base camps in northern Mexico. One dispatch rider, Juan Gallego, made the trip back and forth five times. The riders carried letters and other news from New Spain.

A letter written by Coronado to the Spanish king had the tone of an apology: "What I am sure of is that there is not any gold nor any other metal in all this country, [there] are nothing but little villages. . . . I have done all that I possibly could to serve your Majesty, and to discover a country where God Our Lord might be served and the royal patrimony of your Majesty increased. . . . The best place I have found is the River of Tiguex (the Rio Grande) where I am now."

A feeling of gloom swept over the men as the winter progressed. They had started the expedition full of hope and high dreams, believing there was treasure for everyone in the northlands. But two years of loneliness, harsh traveling, and constant peril had yielded nothing for the gold-hungry Spaniards. All they had for their efforts were rotting saddles and clothing worn to rags. Worst of all, their bodies were covered with lice that seemed to multiply despite their efforts to get rid of the pests. Because of their despair, the soldiers bickered and fought among each other.

The coming of spring, however, brought a glimmer of hope to the Spaniards. Rumors circulated that the army would make another trip to Quivira and then go beyond that village in search of the golden cities. Perhaps the men might still return to New Spain as rich as lords.

In preparation for another march, the Spaniards exercised their horses. One spring day Coronado, an excellent horseman, joined a group of his officers practicing a military drill called "riding the ring". The commander's servants had put a new strap on his saddle that morning. But the strap, like much of the army's equipment, had become rotten during the long

Kuaua Pueblo in Coronado State Park, Bernalillo, New Mexico. The Bernalillo region was known to Coronado as Tiguex.

journey. While he was riding at full speed, the saddle broke loose and the general was thrown to the ground. The horse then galloped over the rider, giving Coronado a terrible hoof blow to the head. Coronado lay motionless on the ground. Many of his men feared he was dead.

The commander was carried to his bed, where he remained for several days. When he regained consciousness, he told his closest friends of a prophecy told to him by an astrologer before he left Spain. The astrologer predicted Coronado would become a large landowner in a province far from his homeland. But the astrologer added that Coronado was destined to die from a horrible fall, a fall from which he would never recover.

The blow on the head and the recall of the astrologer's prophecy had a powerful effect on Coronado. Previously he had been inclined to try at least one more expedition to the north country. Now, after the accident, he wanted only to go home. He feared he would die without ever seeing his pretty wife again. The thought of breaking trails over more unexplored land suddenly filled him with dread. Home was his only desire—home to New Spain.

Coronado's sudden obsession to return split the camp's officers into two opposing parties. One group wanted to defy the commander and continue exploring. Another group agreed with Coronado and be-

The Rio Grande as it cuts through the heart of New Mexico

lieved it was high time to march south. Captain Juan Jaramillo was one who opposed going back to New Spain. In his narrative of the expedition, Jaramillo hinted that the hoof blow on the head had impaired Coronado's ability to command. "Here [in Tiguex] the general fell from his horse while racing and hurt his head. As a result he showed a mean disposition and plotted the return. Although ten or twelve of us pleaded with him, we were unable to dissuade him."

Coronado's wishes prevailed, and the army began the long retreat from Tiguex in April 1542. Even before the march began, dispatch riders brought disastrous news from northern Mexico. The base camps and outposts Coronado's army established there had been destroyed in a bloody Indian war. Coronado later discovered that the heavy-handed Spanish officers he had chosen to rule the outposts had murdered and tortured the Indians, thereby sparking rebellion. Needless wars brought on by brutal officers were a story sadly familiar to the Coronado mission.

Three of Coronado's priests and some of their assistants decided not to return with the army to New Spain. Instead the missionaries elected to remain in the northland and preach the word of Christ to the Indians there.

It is generally believed that all three priests were killed shortly after the army departed. Many Indian people revered the friars, but others looked upon them as representatives of an enemy race that waged war, killed wantonly, and stole winter provisions. The exact fate of two of the priests is unknown, but there were witnesses to the death of Father Juan de Padilla. The subsequent travels of those witnesses rivaled the adventures of Cabeza de Vaca.

Father Juan de Padilla hiked back to Quivira to preach to the people there. Traveling with Padilla was a Portuguese assistant named Andres Do Campo, and two Mexican priests-in-training. The Quivirans greeted the four men enthusiastically. But while traveling north of Quivira, the party was attacked by Kansa warriors. The priest ordered Do Campo and the two novices to flee. Father Juan de Padilla then waited on his knees, praying, while the Kansa men rushed him. The warriors filled his body with arrows. From a distance, Do Campo and the two novices observed the murder.

Later Do Campo and the novice priests sneaked back to the scene to give Father Padilla a Christian burial. The three men then faced south and began a long and what must have been an adventurous walk. Some five years later, Do Campo and his companions staggered into a northern Mexican village. As was

Juan de Padilla

The desolate Zuni River Valley, along Arizona's Coronado Trail

true with Cabeza de Vaca, the men had been captured and forced to serve for long periods as slaves for various native groups in the American Southwest. Always they escaped, and always they struggled farther south. Had any of the three written an account of their incredible journey, the story would have made them famous. They attempted no such written account, however, and today the pages of history contain little about the amazing travels of Andres Do Campo and the two novice priests.

Coronado's march back over New Mexico and Arizona was unremarkable. The long journey was mostly a matter of retracing the steps taken two years earlier. All the men knew what to expect. This time the vast desert in northern Arizona inspired no fear. Castañeda wrote, "The despoblado was traversed without incident."

An early drawing of Southwestern Indians driving off Spanish soldiers and missionaries

Upon reaching northern Mexico, Coronado discovered an even greater disaster than what he had feared. All the outpost towns his army had built were destroyed by rampaging Indians. Many Spaniards had been killed. The Indians, furious at the horrible treatment given them by Coronado's officers, were on the warpath. Though the Indians did not attack the main army, few Spaniards slept while camped there. The nights were alive with chilling Indian war cries.

As the Spaniards approached Mexico City, Coronado lost control of his once superbly disciplined army. Many soldiers, fearing punishment for their deeds in the north, deserted. Other officers and men openly disobeyed orders from their commander. Castañeda claimed, "Even if the general had wanted [to punish those who disobeyed him], his authority

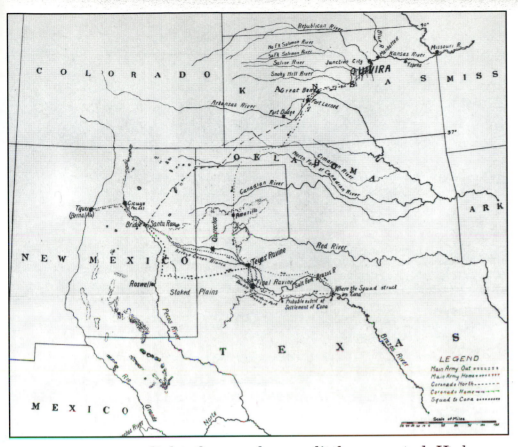

This 1912 map traces Coronado's route from New Mexico to Kansas and back.

was slight, for now he was little respected. He began to be afraid again; and pretending that he was ill, he surrounded himself with guards."

Near New Spain's capital, the army seemed to melt away as the men deserted in droves. At the end of the long journey Coronado commanded fewer than one hundred of the original three hundred Spanish soldiers who began the expedition. Those who remained were hungry, exhausted, and dispirited. Their march had lasted two-and-one-half years, and they had covered more than 6,000 miles (9,656 kilometers) of mostly unexplored territory. Never once had they lost a battle with an Indian foe. Yet, from the standpoint of Spanish military tradition, they returned in disgrace. Instead of achieving God, gold, and glory, they limped back empty-handed.

Chapter 10
The Aftermath

At the same time Coronado trekked over the American Southwest, another Spanish army, led by Hernando De Soto, explored what is now the southern states. Elements of the De Soto party marched as far west as the Texas border in 1542, bringing them just a few hundred miles from Coronado's men. In one of the era's surprising coincidences, an Indian woman actually met both groups of Europeans in the southwestern wilderness. The woman had been a slave at Tiguex, where she encountered Coronado's party. She escaped from her Tiguex masters and journeyed south and east until she accidentally stumbled into the De Soto camp. The chances of her meeting the only two European exploring parties in the entire American Southwest seem almost impossible, but the De Soto records claim the encounters took place.

De Soto's journey lasted three years and his men crossed what are now the states of Florida, Georgia, South Carolina, North Carolina, Tennessee, Alabama, Mississippi, Arkansas, Texas, and possibly Louisiana. The Spaniards under De Soto also found no treasure. The failures of the Coronado and De Soto missions to gather gold dampened Spanish enthusiasm about the lands north of New Spain. Some sixty years passed before Spanish authorities once more sent a major expedition to the northern regions.

The great march to the northland ended Coronado's career as an explorer. Upon his return, he once again assumed the post of governor of New Galicia. By this time, New Galicia's capital had been moved to the booming frontier town of Guadalajara. Once settled in his new home there, Coronado was a devoted husband to Doña Beatríz and a caring father to their two

Hernando De Soto

daughters. Soon, however, Spanish officials began questioning the conduct of Coronado's men.

Coronado's lieutenant, López de Cárdenas, who had burned Indians at the stake, was called to Madrid to stand trial. Charges against him included "perpetrating robberies, burnings, cruelties, and many other offenses against the native Indians of the lands through which he passed." Cárdenas argued that all of his actions were taken during the heat of battle. The court refused to accept his defense, and Cárdenas spent more than seven years in jail for his crimes.

Because he, too, was accused of committing crimes during the mission, Coronado was removed from his post as New Galicia's governor and ordered to Mexico City to stand trial. A Spanish investigator claimed Coronado committed "great cruelties upon the natives of the land through which he passed." After lengthy discussions, the Mexico City court found Coronado innocent of any wrongdoing.

But scandals connected with the expedition tarnished Coronado's reputation, and he never again attained a powerful position of leadership in New Spain. Coronado and his family moved to Mexico City in the 1540s. There he maintained his friendship with Viceroy Mendoza, who made him a minor official in city government. As he carried out his duties, Coronado was known for his efficiency and his clocklike regularity in keeping appointments.

While living in Mexico City, Coronado had many bouts with serious illness. His friends believed the hoof blow he received while riding in Tiguex had destroyed his health. Coronado died in 1554, twelve years after he completed his historic journey. At the time of his death he was forty-four years old.

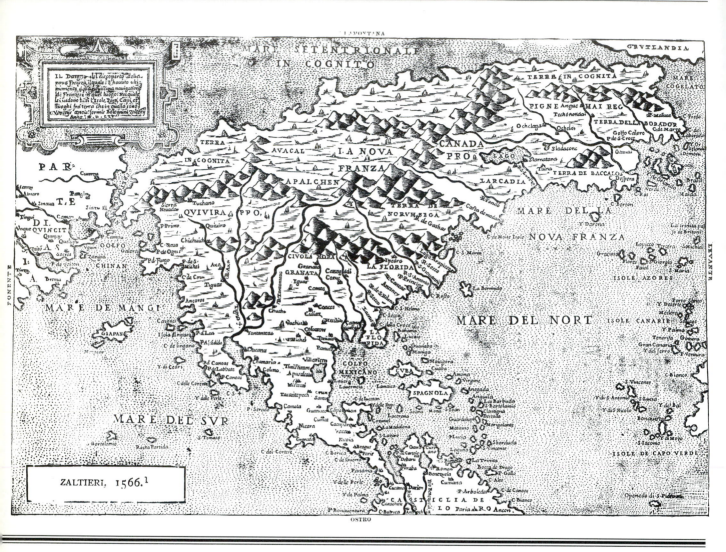

ZALTIERI, 1566.[1]

In this map, a sixteenth-century Italian geographer tried to include as many points in North America as he had heard of.

Though he had not discovered the great cities of gold, Coronado's journey added to the European vision of the North American continent. Early in the age of exploration, the Europeans believed North America to be a long and narrow land mass. Thanks to Coronado, they began to appreciate the continent's width. After his mission, European-drawn maps improved tremendously. And for the next hundred years, Spanish mapmakers included two tiny dots in the center of the North American continent: Cíbola and Tiguex.

Coronado's achievements as an explorer are matched by few other men of his era. He and his followers marched out of northern Mexico and journeyed through areas that are now Arizona, New Mexico, Texas, Oklahoma, Kansas, and perhaps as far north as Nebraska. Their passage led them through rich pine forests, stark deserts, and wild mountain passes. They were the first Europeans to see the Grand Canyon, the Painted Desert, the Great Plains, and the herds of buffalo so large they defied the imagination. The Coronado expedition was truly one of the most fantastic adventures in the history of exploration.

The Indian known as the Turk leading Coronado and his men in their grand quest for Quivira

Relacion de la jor-
nada de Cibola, con-
puesta por Pedro de
Castañeda de Naçe-
ra donde se trata de
todos aquellos pobla-
dos y ritos, y costumbres, la qual fue
el Año de 1540

Opposite page: Title page from a journal of Coronado's expedition, written by Pedro de Castañeda, one of Coronado's soldiers

Above: First page of Castañeda's journal

Timeline of Events in Coronado's Lifetime

1510—Francisco Vásquez de Coronado is born in Salamanca, Spain; explorer Vasco Núñez de Balboa lands in present-day Panama

1513—Balboa discovers the Pacific Ocean

1519—Explorer Hernando Cortés sails to Mexico's Yucatan Peninsula and begins his conquest of Mexico; Ferdinand Magellan begins his voyage around the world

1521—Cortés conquers Mexico's Aztecs, beginning Spain's colonial empire in Mexico; Magellan is killed in a Pacific island battle

1528—Alvar Núñez Cabeza de Vaca makes an expedition to Florida; shipwrecked off the Texas coast, he hikes westward through what is now the American Southwest

1535—With Viceroy Antonio de Mendoza, Coronado goes to New Spain (Mexico) and makes a home in Mexico City

1536—Cabeza de Vaca reports rumors of riches to the Spaniards in Mexico

1537—Coronado marries Doña Beatríz de Estrada, by whom he eventually has two daughters

1538—Viceroy Mendoza names Coronado governor of the province of New Galicia

1539—Mendoza sends the friar Marcos de Niza and the slave Estéban on an expedition to locate the fabled Seven Cities of Cíbola; Estéban is killed, but de Niza sees a city he believes to be Cíbola

1540—Coronado embarks on his journey into northern Mexico, Arizona, and New Mexico; he battles Indians at Cíbola, then sends out four expeditionary parties: Pedro de Tovar enters Hopi territory; García López de Cárdenas sees the Grand Canyon; Melchor Díaz marches west to the Colorado River and into southern California; Hernando de Alvarado explores north and east, arriving in Tiguex, north of present-day Albuquerque, New Mexico; Mendoza sends Hernando de Alarcón up the Gulf of California, where he discovers the mouth of the Colorado River

1540-1541—Coronado travels to Tiguex, where the Spaniards assault and execute many Indians and eventually defeat them

1541—Seeking the land of Quivira, Coronado marches into the Great Plains, crossing the present-day Texas and Oklahoma panhandles and entering Kansas

1542—Hernando de Soto's expedition travels through what is now the southeastern and southern United States, going as far west as Texas; Coronado returns to New Spain, reports to Mendoza, resumes his governorship of New Galicia, and later holds a seat on the Mexico City council

1545—In Mexico City, Coronado is tried on charges that he mishandled the Cíbola expedition

1546—Coronado is found innocent of wrongdoing

1554—Francisco Vásquez de Coronado dies on September 22 in Mexico City

Glossary of Terms

adobe—A building material made of clay and straw

artillery—Weapons such as bows, cannons, or catapults that launch objects through the air

assault—To attack physically or with words

astrologer—A person who claims to tell the future by observing planets and stars

atrocities—Cruel or brutal acts

avalanche—A sudden rush of earth, rocks, or snow down a mountainside; any similar downpour of objects

awl—A tool for piercing holes in leather

bastion—A stronghold or fortified area

boulders—Huge rocks

casualties—People killed or seriously wounded in battle

colossal—Enormous, huge, gigantic

commodities—Valuable farming or mining products

confiscate—To take someone's property away through government or military authority

conspiracy—A plot

contingent—A group of representatives or delegates

defuse—To calm a situation, as if removing the fuse from an explosive

dispatch riders—Speedy riders sent off to deliver messages

domesticated—Tamed

edifice—A building

extol—To praise or glorify something's virtues

famished—Hungry, starving

fanatical—Extremely enthusiastic or devoted

feral animal—A wild, untamed animal

feudal lord—In medieval times, a powerful landowner with tenants who work the land, serve him, and pay him homage

fording a river—Walking across a river at a shallow point

freebooter—Someone who goes to war or goes on a mission in order to gain wealth

friction—Conflict between people who oppose each other

giddiness—Feverish excitement

gourd—A squash whose outer shell can be hollowed out and used as a utensil or decoration

infernal—Damnable; relating to hell

interpreter—Someone who understands and translates a different language

ironic—Having features that contradict each other

lice—Tiny, wingless insects that attach themselves to humans and animals, causing itching and skin irritation

massacre—A battle in which a great number of people are cruelly killed

meander—To travel in a winding, wandering course

medieval—Relating to the Middle Ages, a period in European history lasting from about A.D. 500 through 1500

metropolis—A large, important city

mirage—An optical illusion in which the eyes see water in the desert where there is none; any false appearance of something desirable that is not really there

nomadic—Roaming from place to place; not settled in one location

odyssey—A long journey full of extraordinary events

panhandle—A narrow section of a territory extending out from its main body of land

patrimony—Property inherited from one's father; property that belongs to a king or a church

perpetrate—Commit; carry out

point man—A soldier sent out ahead of his fellow troops; anyone who moves forward in advance of others

ramrod—A stiff rod for cleaning a gun or loading ammunition into it

resplendent—Dazzling, glistening, gleaming

retaliatory—Done in revenge; done to get even

sedentary—Settled in one location

sediment—Soil, rocks, or minerals that are carried along by flowing water and settle to the bottom of a river or lake

siege—A prolonged attack that wears down the opponent

sinews—Tendons

technicolor—Colored like a color movie

terraced—Carved or built in step-like banks

titanic—Large, forceful, or powerful

treacherous—Unreliable, likely to betray, presenting a danger

trek—A difficult expedition on foot or by wagon

truce—An agreement to stop fighting

viceroy—Someone who rules a region as the representative of a king

Bibliography

For further reading, see:

Bolton, Herbert E. *Coronado, Knight of Pueblos and Plains*. Albuquerque: University of New Mexico Press, 1981.

Campbell, Camilla. *Coronado and His Captains*. Chicago: Follett Publishing Company, 1958. For younger readers.

Day, A. Grove. *Coronado and the Discovery of the Southwest*. Des Moines, IA: Meredith, 1967. For younger readers.

Day, A. Grove. *Coronado's Quest: Discovery of the Southwestern States*. Westport, CN: Greenwood Press, 1982. Reprint of 1964 edition.

Hammond, George P., editor. *Narratives of the Coronado Expedition, 1540-1542*. NY: AMS Press, 1975. Reprint of 1940 edition.

Syme, Ronald. *Francisco Coronado and the Seven Cities of Gold*. NY: William Morrow and Company, 1965. For younger readers.

Udall, Stewart L. *To the Inland Empire: Coronado and Our Spanish Legacy*. Garden City, NY: Doubleday, 1987.

Index

Page numbers in boldface type indicate illustrations.

Picture Identifications for Chapter Opening Spreads

6-7—View of Mexico across the Rio Grande River at Big Bend National Park, Texas
10-11—Cathedral and Roman bridge at Salamanca, Spain
18-19—Desert scenery near Hermosillo in Sonora, Mexico
30-31—Bonito Creek in the White Mountains on Arizona's Fort Apache Indian Reservation
44-45—Indian paintbrush along the Santa Fe Trail near Fort Union, New Mexico
56-57—Dawn at Organ Pipe Cactus National Monument, Arizona; Diaz Peak and Spire in the background were named for Melchor Díaz
74-75—Kiva mural at Kuaua Pueblo in Coronado State Park, Bernalillo, New Mexico
86-87—Spring thunderstorm near Lyons, Kansas
102-103—Sunset, Saguaro National Monument, Arizona
112-113—Desert vegetation in Grand Canyon National Park

Acknowledgment

For a critical reading of the manuscript, our thanks to John Parker, Ph.D., Curator Emeritus, James Ford Bell Library, University of Minnesota, Minneapolis, Minnesota.

Picture Acknowledgments

Bill Ahrendt—2
The Bettmann Archive—5, 117
Brown Brothers—33, 108
© **Reinhard Brucker**—28, 51 (top), 89, 102-103, 106
Marilyn Gartman Agency: © Audrey Gibson—66
© **Virginia R. Grimes**—81
Historical Pictures Service, Chicago—12, 20, 24, 32, 42, 77, 110
Institute of Texan Cultures, San Antonio—21, 27, 29
© **Jerry Jacka**—30-31, 36, 37, 39, 40, 51 (bottom), 56-57, 59, 60, 61, 63, 65, 69, 70, 71, 76, 79, 85, 86-87, 95, 98, 99, 109
Kansas State Historical Society, Topeka—96, 97, 111
© **Kirkendall/Spring**—112-113
Len Meents—64
Courtesy of Museum of New Mexico, Santa Fe—9 (#20206), 48 (#48918)
Courtesy of New Mexico State Records Center and Archives, Santa Fe—118, 119
North Wind Picture Archives—17, 22, 41, 43, 47, 49, 53, 54, 78, 90, 91, 92, 93, 114, 116
© **North Wind Pictures**—44-45, 52, 74-75, 83, 101, 105
Odyssey Productions: © Robert Frerck—10-11, 13, 14, 18-19, 35
© **Pecos National Historical Park, Pecos, New Mexico**—80
Chip and Rosa Maria Peterson—16
Root Resources: © Kenneth W. Fink—88
Permanent Collection, The Roswell Museum and Art Center, Roswell, New Mexico—82
Archives Division, Texas State Library, Austin—8
Tom Stack & Associates: © Tom Algire—4; © Don & Pat Valenti—73
SuperStock—55
Valan Photos: © Kennon Cooke—6-7, 23

About the Author

R. Conrad Stein was born and grew up in Chicago. He attended the University of Illinois, where he earned a degree in history. He later earned an advanced degree from the University of Guanajuato in Mexico. Mr. Stein now lives in Chicago with his wife and his daughter Janna. The study of history, particularly the history of Mexico, fascinates Mr. Stein. To prepare for this book he travelled to the Southwest and retraced Coronado's route through Arizona, New Mexico, and beyond.